AMERICAN COSMIC

AMERICAN COSMIC

UFOs, Religion, Technology

D. W. PASULKA

OXFORD
UNIVERSITY PRESS

OXFORD
UNIVERSITY PRESS

Oxford University Press is a department of the University of Oxford. It furthers the University's objective of excellence in research, scholarship, and education by publishing worldwide. Oxford is a registered trade mark of Oxford University Press in the UK and certain other countries.

Published in the United States of America by Oxford University Press
198 Madison Avenue, New York, NY 10016, United States of America.

© Oxford University Press 2019

Parts of Chapter Four have been adapted from D. W. Pasulka's article
"The Fairy Tale is True": Social Technologies of the Religious
Supernatural in Film and New Media in the Journal of the American
Academy of Religion, Volume 84, Issue 2, 1 June 2016, Pages 530–547.
Used with Permission.

Library of Congress Cataloging-in-Publication Data
Names: Pasulka, D. W., author.
Title: American cosmic : UFOs, religion, techonology.
Description: New York, NY : Oxford University Press, [2019] | Includes index.
Identifiers: LCCN 2018015547 (print) | LCCN 2018047070 (ebook) |
ISBN 9780190693497 (updf) | ISBN 9780190693503 (epub) |
ISBN 9780190692889 (hardcover)
Subjects: LCSH: Unidentified flying objects—Religious aspects. |
Unidentified flying objects in popular culture. | Life on other
planets—Religious aspects. | Extraterrestrial beings in popular culture.
Classification: LCC BL65.U54 (ebook) |
LCC BL65.U54 P37 2019 (print) | DDC 001.9420973—dc23
LC record available at https://lccn.loc.gov/2018015547

9 8 7 6 5 4 3 2 1

Printed by Sheridan Books, Inc., United States of America

American Cosmic is dedicated to Tyler.

"Almost two thousand years, and no new god!"

—FRIEDRICH NIETZSCHE

"The Internet is an alien life form."

—DAVID BOWIE

CONTENTS

PREFACE

*A Tour of Silicon Valley
with Jacques Vallee*

"These are the hills of Silicon Valley. There are many secrets in this valley."

Jacques Vallee maneuvers his car expertly through the daunting San Francisco Bay Area traffic, darting this way and that. Large trucks and small cars barrel toward us on the winding roads, and crashes are narrowly evaded. Every twenty minutes I lift my shoulders, which are stuck to the back of the car seat, and try to shake out the tension.

Jacques, father of the modern study of UFOs and an early visionary of the internet, is giving me and my colleague, Robbie Graham, a personal tour of his favorite geolocation, Silicon Valley. We drive by places that loom large in the history of "the Valley." He recalls the early days of the technology revolution: "They were on fire and purely democratic. Pure scientists, fueled by discovery." Jacques's credentials are intimidating. As an astronomer, he helped NASA create the first detailed map of Mars. As a computer scientist with a

PhD from Northwestern University, he was one of the early engineers of ARPANET, the Advanced Research Projects Agency, a precursor of the internet. He is also a successful venture capitalist, funding startups of innovative technologies that have changed the daily lives of millions of people. He is a prolific author. He is probably most famous for being a consultant to Steven Spielberg on the movie *Close Encounters of the Third Kind* (1977). The scientist character in the movie, played by French actor François Truffaut, is based on Jacques. Jacques has perhaps done more for the field of ufology than anyone else in its short history, and yet he calls the study of UFOs his hobby.

This is the orthodox history of Jacques's life and work. His unorthodox history is equally interesting. He worked with scientists affiliated with the Stanford Research Institute, now SRI International, an independent, nonprofit research institute in Menlo Park. The group's activities are largely unknown to the public, but declassified documents from the 1970s and 1980s indicate that it was a research site for the extraordinary. Jacques did his early work on the internet under a program that, as Jeffrey Kripal writes, was probably called "Augmentation of the Human Intellect."

This research was happening at the same time and in the same place as studies of remote viewing, precognition, and extrasensory perception. These esoteric skills were studied under a classified program called The Stargate Project, funded by the US military in partnership with the SRI. The hope was that the skills and talents of people who were naturally psychic could be developed and harnessed for the purposes of gathering intelligence. In the course of this research, the psychic viewers reportedly uncovered unintended and surprising targets, like UFOs. The participants in the program also reported that they could travel through space, to the moon, and to other planets, like Mars. In other words, the program allegedly developed, intentionally or not, psychic cosmonauts.

Perhaps unknown to Jacques and the researchers of the SRI, psychic travel had long been reported. Psychic cosmonauts like the eighteenth-century philosopher/theologian Emanuel Swedenborg crop up throughout the history of religions. Swedenborg claimed that, with the assistance of an angel, he had visited Mercury, Mars, Venus, and the moon. He claimed to have spoken to beings on those planets and he published his experiences in a book, *Life on Other Planets* (1758). The activities of the cosmonauts of the SRI may have resembled the interstellar adventures of Swedenborg, but their goals could not have been more different. They hoped to operationalize the knowledge they acquired about terrestrial targets; remote viewing was one of many methods of attempted data collection. These efforts to create human portals to other planets were taking place under the same auspices and at the same time as technologies of connectivity like the internet.

As we spun down the highway, I recognized the neighborhoods of my childhood, but I saw them now through Jacques's eyes. The streets, the smell of the eucalyptus trees, parks, schools, cafes—all looked new to me, shining with the allure of mystery. As much as I wanted to, I never got up the nerve to ask Jacques exactly what he meant by the secrets of Silicon Valley. But on that drive I caught a glimpse into the exciting ideology and philosophy behind the revolution—its zeitgeist.

If Jacques were an essay, he would be "The Question Concerning Technology" by the philosopher Martin

Heidegger. This essay, dubbed impenetrable by many readers, nevertheless offers several intriguing observations about the relationship between humans and technology. As Heidegger saw it, humans do not understand the essence of technology. Instead, they are blinded by it and view it simply as an instrument. The interpretation of technology as pure instrumentality was wrong, he said. The Greek temple, for the Greeks, housed the gods, and as such it was a sacred "frame." Similarly, the medieval cathedral embodied and housed the presence of God for medieval Europeans. Heidegger suggested that the human relationship with technology is religiouslike, that it is possible for us to have a noninstrumental relationship with technology and engage fully with what it really is: a saving power. Jacques Vallee is fully aware of the revolution that is technology. Although he most likely never read Heidegger's essay, Jacques's depiction of Silicon Valley as the home of the new resonates with Heidegger's vision of technology as bringing to birth a new era of human experience, a new epoch.

The symbol for this new epoch is the UFO. Carl Jung called the UFO a technological angel. This is a book about UFOs and technology, but also about a group of people who believe anomalous technology functions as creative inspiration. I found these people. In the 1970s, when Jacques consulted on *Close Encounters*, he encouraged Spielberg to portray the more complex version of the story, that is, that the phenomenon is complex and might not be extraterrestrial at all. But Spielberg went with the simple story, the one everybody would understand. He said, "This is Hollywood." This book does not tell the simple story, but I believe it is a story anyone can understand.

ACKNOWLEDGMENTS

I am indebted to those who helped me in the process of writing this book, which has been an adventure from the beginning. More than an adventure, the research has brought me into a deep relationship with the forces that motivated me, as a child and young adult, to study religion.

I am indebted to Jeffrey Kripal and Michael Murphy for supporting my effort to explore religion and technology. Jeff has been a great mentor to many scholars whose work seeks to grapple with religious experience, and his integrity and courage have innovated the study of religion in ground-breaking ways. His work continues to be an inspiration to me.

I would like to thank my editor, Cynthia Read, whose suggestions and book recommendations were always serendipitous and relevant. Early on in my research Cynthia suggested I read Dr. George M. Young's *The Russian Cosmists: The Esoteric Futurism of Nikolai Fedorov and His Followers*. I received the book as I was researching the history of the American space program, and as I interviewed scientists whose intimate relationships with rockets and satellites could have been the content for the next chapter in Dr. Young's book. Dr. Young's work on the esoteric traditions of the Russian space program was so relevant to my work that my title, *American Cosmic*, is an homage to his brilliant book.

I am indebted to Christopher Bledsoe and his wife, Yvonne, and to the whole Bledsoe family. Their kindness and hospitality allowed me a peek into the blessings and hardships that an experience can produce on a person and his or her family members. I wish to thank Chad Hayes and Carey Hayes, whom I worked with as a religion consultant for *The Conjuring* franchise. They were open to my academic proclivities and allowed me to view the making of a media production about the supernatural from the inside.

Whitley Strieber's work and friendship helped me understand aspects of the phenomenon that are not easily understood. Whitley's brilliant commentaries, insights, help, and moral support were instrumental in helping me finish the book manuscript. I would like to thank my colleagues Brenda Denzler, who donated her library of UFO-related materials to me, and Dr. David Halperin, whose inspiring work on the topic of UFOs is brilliant and helped me think through my own work. I am grateful to Rey Hernandez and to astronaut Edgar Mitchell for their insights and helpfulness with my section on quantum physics and Rey's experience. Nancy Mullis and Kary Mullis were both kind, very helpful, and deeply insightful. I wish to thank them for their friendship. Tanya Luhrmann's work and comments were very helpful and always brilliant.

I would like to thank Jacques Vallee, whose work and insights permeate this book. My thanks to him cannot be overstated, as his ideas about the phenomenon and technology have proved to be prescient. I owe so much to my anonymous friends, Tyler D. and James. They possess a burning desire to know the mystery, and I was infected with their enthusiasm.

I am indebted to researchers Scott Browne, Allison Kruse, and David Stinnett. Scott's Facebook page, *In the Field*, provides a forum for serious videographers to vet their captures, and Scott, to his credit, has kept the forum free from the vitriol that accompanies much discussion within ufology. I owe thanks to my friend Robbie Graham, who early in my research helped me think through a lot of the theoretical aspects of the phenomenon, and to Greg Bishop, whose own work on the topic helped me to understand the climate of the research. George Hansen's work was instrumental in helping me understand the "trickster" element of the phenomenon. Dr. Patty Turrisi, my colleague and friend, provided moral support and helpful comments. Dr. Dean Radin's work, and his comments, were helpful and always fascinating. I met many virtual but nonetheless real friends during this research, including David Metcalfe, whose insights into digital technology have been instrumental to putting together several helpful pieces of the puzzle. Christopher Laursen has been a wonderful conversation partner throughout the experience. My students have inspired me with their intelligence and bravery. They include Jose Herrera, Steve Nunez, Lauryn Justice, Bryan Hendershot, Eugene O'Dea, and so many others. My student Alex Karas was instrumental in helping me as a research assistant, and I am especially thankful for his help.

I want to thank my wonderful family, especially my little brother. As latchkey kids we used to sit in our living room with the neighbor kids watching rerun episodes of the *Twilight Zone*, never anticipating that one day, we would wake up in an actual episode.

AMERICAN COSMIC

INTRODUCTION

When you gaze long into the abyss, the abyss gazes
also into you.

—FRIEDRICH NIETZSCHE

AS I FINISH WRITING THIS INTRODUCTION, the television
series *60 Minutes* has just aired an interview with billionaire
Robert Bigelow, of Bigelow Aerospace. Bigelow founded his
company, which specializes in manufactured space equipment, mostly with his own funding in 1998. Due to the reli-
ability and safety of Bigelow Aerospace's equipment, NASA
and other space companies use Bigelow's space habitats and
other equipment in their explorations and experiments in
space. In the interview, Bigelow boldly claimed that aliens, or
nonhuman intelligences, are interacting with humans, and
have been for a long time.

"Is it risky for you to say in public that you believe in
UFOs and aliens?" asked interviewer Lara Logan. "You don't
worry that some people will say, 'Did you hear that guy? He
sounds like he's crazy'?"

"I don't give a damn. I don't care," Bigelow replied. "It's
not going to make a difference. It's not going to change the
reality of what I know."[1]

I was not surprised by Bigelow's statements. They are
typical of the many scientist-believers I have met since
I began my research in 2012. Since that time, I have come

to know millionaires and billionaires and successful innovative scientists who believe in and study the phenomenon. This was the first of several surprising revelations about the UFO phenomenon. People like Stephen Hawking are wrong when they state, as Hawking did in his 2008 TED Talk, "I am discounting reports of UFOs. Why would they appear to only cranks and weirdos?"[2] The lie has been that belief in UFOs is associated with those on the "fringe"—"cranks and weirdos," in Hawking's words. The truth is just the opposite.

This book is about contemporary religion, using as a case study the phenomenon known as the UFO. It is also about technology. These may seem like completely unrelated topics, but they are intimately connected. They are connected because social and economic infrastructures shape the ways in which people practice religions. A historical and uncontroversial example is the impact of the printing press on the Christian tradition. The mass production of Bibles in the common languages of the people soon gave rise to the doctrine of *Sola Scriptura*, or Scripture Alone, according to which scripture is the only reliable and necessary guide for Christian faith and practice—a foundational principle of the Protestant Reformation. As technologies shift infrastructures, religious practices and habits are changed.

Beyond documenting how technological infrastructure shapes religious practices and beliefs, the UFO is considered by believers *to be* advanced technology. Like the Spiritualists of the nineteenth century, believers see technology as a portal or a frequency shift that allows humans to connect to other minds, human or extraterrestrial, as well as to places outside of the current understanding of space-time.[3] Therefore, not only is the technological infrastructure the basis for widespread belief in UFOs, through media technologies and other mechanisms, but also technology *itself* is a sacred medium, as well as the sacred object, of this new religiosity. Conversely, within certain theological circles, technology, especially the internet, has been characterized as "the Beast," the anti-Christ. Technology in these contexts is not secular but infused with theological meaning.

A UNIQUE EXPERIENCE FOR AN ACADEMIC

This book is about how technology informs a widespread and growing religiosity focused on UFOs, but it is also a story. It is partly the story of my own participation in a group of scientists and academics who study the phenomenon anonymously (except for me, of course). The participants are anonymous because of the stigma that is often associated with UFOs and belief in them, but also because there were classified government programs in which the phenomenon was studied, necessitating secrecy among the participants. To offset any conspiratorial interpretations of this book, I will clarify that I am not "read in" to any government program to study the phenomenon, I was never privy to any classified information of which I am aware, nor am I part of an official or nonofficial disclosure of UFOs to the American public.

I began my study of UFO cultures in January 2012. I proceeded in the conventional way in that I conducted an ethnography of a variety of believers and delved into research into UFOs and ufology, a branch of research devoted to the topic. I was lucky to inherit an extensive library of resources about UFOs and reports of contactees/experiencers from Dr. Brenda Denzler, whose own book, *The Lure of the*

Edge, informed my study. The library included her own research, as well as the research of ufologists and organizations like MUFON (the Mutual UFO Network) and CUFOS (Center for UFO Studies) and the works of other academics and researchers studying the phenomenon. I read the works of Allen Hynek, Jacques Vallee, John Keel, Budd Hopkins, and John Mack, as well as those of people who theorize the phenomenon academically, such as Jeffrey Kripal, Whitley Strieber, Debbora Battaglia, Greg Eghigian, Carole Cusack, Susan Lepsetter, and David Halperin.

Not long after I began, I quickly surmised that there is a parallel research tradition within the field of the study of the phenomenon, and that there always has been. There are public ufologists who are known for their work, there are a few academics who write about the topic, and then there is an "Invisible College," as Allen Hynek called it and of which Jacques Vallee wrote—a group of scientists, academics, and others who will never make their work public, or at least not for a long time, although the results of their investigations impact society in many ways. Halfway through my research I made the decision to write about this group, for a couple of reasons. First, they receive no recognition or press, yet rumors about them spawn folklore and traditions that constitute the UFO narrative. Second, frankly, this was the group whose work and members I became best acquainted with, and whose stories I found most fascinating. I had to muster courage to write about this group because its members are anonymous, and what I observed of their work places me in the odd position of *almost* confirming a myth. This is not the preferred position of the academic author of books about religion. It is usually the place occupied by authors of theology. In the end, however, I chose the path of writing a book that conveys what I consider the most interesting, and challenging, aspects about the topic.

The parallel tradition of ufology is not known to the uninitiated, but it is well known within the culture of ufologists. Some scientists, such as astronomer Massimo Teodorani and physicist Eric Davis, have confirmed its existence. Teodorani writes:

> I have been quite heavily involved in the so called "ufo" stuff for at least 25 years, in research that is parallel to more canonic studies of physics and astronomy. I know that some anomalies do exist and I stress the importance of studying this problem scientifically, especially when measurement instruments are used. For many years I have been studying the problem behind totally closed doors.[4]

Davis has also noted this aspect of the study of UFOs. "UFOs are real phenomena," he writes. "They are artificial objects under intelligent control. They're definitely craft of a supremely advanced technology." He goes on to say that most of what academics and scientists know about the phenomenon is secret, and will probably remain so. "There are scientists who are aware of evidence and observational data that is not refutable. It is absolutely corroborated, using forensic techniques and methodology. But they won't come out and publicize that because they fear it. Not the subject—they fear the backlash from their professional colleagues." He notes that one tradition of study requires secrecy, as it is related to the military: "It's the domain of military science. The fact that [unknown] craft are flying around Earth is not a subject for science—it is a subject for intelligence gathering collection and analysis."[5]

There are a number of players in this story. For the most part, they fall into one of two categories: there are those who engage with and interact with what they believe are nonhuman intelligences, perhaps extraterrestrial or even interdimensional. The people in this category who are featured in this book are the scientists to whom Davis refers. They agreed to be included on condition that they remain anonymous. The second category consists of those who interpret, spin, produce, and market the story of UFO events to the general public. Members of the first category are silent about their research, while members of the second category are very vocal about information they have received second-, third-, or even fourth-hand. Often they even make up stories or derive their information from hoaxes.

The second of the surprising revelations is that even as some respected scientists believe in the phenomenon associated with UFOs and make discoveries about it, what is ultimately marketed to the public about the phenomenon barely resembles these scientists' findings. Belief in the phenomenon is at an all-time high—even among successful, high-profile people like Bigelow. Among those who report sightings are former US president Jimmy Carter and legions of other credible witnesses, including the trained observers of the US Air Force, pilots, commercial pilots, police officers, US Army personnel, and millions of civilians who were certainly not out looking for UFOs.[6] Different polls record varying levels of belief in UFOs, but all indicate that it is pervasive. A 2008 Scripps poll showed that more than 50 percent of Americans believe in extraterrestrial life. Seventy-four percent of people between the ages of eighteen and twenty-four are believers.[7] In 2012, in connection with marketing their UFO-themed programming, National Geographic conducted an informal poll of Americans about their belief in UFOs. They randomly sampled 1,114 individuals over the age of eighteen and found that 36 percent believed UFOs exist and, more significantly, 77 percent believed that there are signs suggesting that aliens have been to Earth in the past. Although not a formal poll, the results concur with professional polls such as the Harris Poll conducted in 2009, which found that 32 percent of Americans believe in UFOs.

I began my own research into aerial phenomena after I finished a book on the Catholic doctrine of purgatory. The project was a multiyear study in which I examined many primary sources of European Catholic history, found mostly in obscure archives, of anecdotes about souls from purgatory. These sources dated from 1300 to 1880. In them I found a lot of other unexpected things, such as reports of orbs of light, flames that penetrated walls, luminous beings, forms of conscious light, spinning suns, and disclike aerial objects. I wasn't sure how to theorize these reports, and I left them out of my book. Yet I wondered about them. I wondered aloud one morning while drinking coffee with a friend.

"These reports remind me of a Steven Spielberg film. You know, lots of shining aerial phenomena, luminous beings, transformed lives," he said.

I summarily dismissed his comparison. The next day, he found an ad for a local conference about UFOs and extraterrestrials taking place the following weekend. He suggested that I attend.

The conference featured speakers who were experiencers, people who have sighted UFOs or believe they have seen extraterrestrials. They described some of the same things I had observed in my research in Catholic history—shining aerial discs, flames, and orbs—and especially how these experiences transformed their lives. The experiencers interpreted these as spiritual or religious events. They either fractured their traditional religious belief systems or, more commonly, caused them to reinterpret their traditions through a biblical–UFO framework in which they viewed biblical and historical religious events as UFO events. Ezekiel's wheel is the prime example of how scripture is used in this context. Many religious practitioners view the strange spinning aerial contraption witnessed by the biblical prophet Ezekiel as a UFO. The television show *Ancient Aliens* offers a similar interpretive slant. This way of looking at anomalous ancient aerial phenomena is not restricted to experiencers but is common, especially among youth such as my students.[8]

Could the orbs of the past, once interpreted as souls from purgatory, still be around? Are they currently being interpreted as UFOs? This question was not so mind-bending. I could still fit this data into my academic training, interpreting orbs as social constructions based on an externally generated unknown event, or some type of perennial mystical experience interpreted through each era's reigning cultural framework.

The challenge began when I met the meta-experiencers, the scientists who studied the experiencers and the phenomenon. It confounded the academic categories I had been using thus far in my work. The new research compelled me to think in novel ways to understand this group and their research. Additionally, the charisma and conviction of the scientist-believers were difficult to discount—at least for me. As a scholar of religion I am trained not to weigh in, one way or the other, on the truth or falseness of believers' claims. When looking at the documentation of the proliferation of a belief, there is no need to consider whether the belief is justified or not if one is just analyzing its social effects and influence. My association with the scientists brought about something that Harvard UFO researcher John Mack called an "epistemological shock," that is, a shock to my fundamental understanding of the world and the universe.

The shock to my epistemological frameworks, or to what I believed to be true, occurred on two levels. The first is obvious. Several of the most well-regarded scientists in the world believe in nonhuman intelligence that originated in space. The second level of epistemological shock was galling. Rumors of the findings of these scientists inspired hoaxes, disinformation, media, and documentaries based on bogus information that purported to inform the public about UFO events and created UFO narratives and mythologies. I watched several of these unfold in real time. It was hard to remain aloof when confronted by what I knew to be misinformation, some created as disinformation, some created for the sole reason that it sells. I was so embedded in the research, on the one level of observing the scientists and on another level of being involved with the producers of media content, that it was impossible to be neutral. It was at this point that I felt myself fall headlong into Nietzsche's abyss, stare into it, and see it grin mockingly back at me.

METHOD

In one sense, I feel as if I have been studying this phenomenon my whole life, but I didn't call it UFO research; I called it religious studies. Scholars of religion are well suited to study this topic because religious studies is not a religion, but a set of methods for studying religious phenomena. With a few exceptions, scholars of religion do not assess the truth claims of religious practitioners. The metaphysical truth and the objective truth of the phenomena are bracketed so that one can focus on the social effects, which are incontestably very real. This strategy is helpful in the study of the phenomenon of UFOs and was advocated by Jacques Vallee in a 1979 address to the special political committee of the United Nations organization. He told the committee that "the belief in space visitors is independent of the physical reality of the UFO phenomenon." Significantly, Vallee himself believes in the reality of the UFO phenomenon but understands that the formation of mass belief in it does not depend on its objective reality.[9]

A NEW RELIGIOUS FORM

It is an understatement to say that in 2012, as soon as my research focus shifted, so did my life. When I began to focus on modern reports of UFO sightings and events, I was immediately immersed in a world where the religious impulse was alive and the formation of a new, unique form of religion was in process. I was observing it as it happened. Carl Jung put it well. Referring to the modern phenomenon of flying saucers, he wrote, "We have here a golden opportunity of seeing how a legend is formed."[10]

The cast of characters who showed up, unannounced and unexpected, surprised me. They included television producers, experiencers and their entourages of agents affiliated with the government, and even actors whose names are known in every household. After my initial shock, I began to understand these individuals from the perspective of the history of religions. In a sense, they were the same cast of characters who appear at the birth of every major religious tradition, although today they have different names and job descriptions. In the first century CE they would be called scribes and redactors, but today they are agents of information, like screenwriters, television producers, and authors. I observed the dynamic genesis of a global belief system. I began to record the mechanisms by which people believe and practice, and *how* they believe and practice. The producers, actors, government agents, and even myself were all part of the process of the formation of belief, and perhaps even pawns in this process.

HOW IS IT RELIGIOUS? THE CONTACT EVENT

One of the scientists with whom I worked, whose methodology is primarily "nuts and bolts" in that he uses scientific analysis on what he believes to be artifacts or physical parts of potential "crafts," asked me why UFO events are often linked to religion. This is a fair question. One answer lies in the fact that the history of religion is, among other things, a record of perceived contact with supernatural beings, many of which descend from the skies as beings of light, or on light, or amid light. This is one of the reasons scholars of religion are comfortable examining modern reports of UFO events. Jeffrey Kripal, working with author Whitely Strieber, articulates this well. In his work he has sought to reveal "how the modern experience of the alien coming down from the sky can be compared to the ancient experience of the god descending from the heavens."[11]

These "contact events," the perceived interface between the human and the intelligent nonhuman being from the sky, spawn beliefs and interpretations. These beliefs and interpretations develop into communities of belief, or faith communities. Kripal notes, "Some of the remembered effects of these fantastic states of mind have been taken up by extremely elaborate social, political, and artistic processes and have been fashioned by communities into mythical, ritual, and institutional complexes that have fundamentally changed human history. We call these 'religions.'"[12]

Similar to religions, institutions appropriate, cultivate, and sometimes intervene in the interpretations of a UFO event. These institutions vary and range from religious institutions to governments to clubs or groups, and, today, to social media groups.

THE FORMATION OF BELIEF COMMUNITIES

In the history of religions, a contact event is followed by a series of interpretations, and these are usually followed by the creation of institutions. Such interpretive communities are often called religions or religious denominations. Institutions have a stake in how the original contact event is interpreted. A familiar example is the communities of interpretation that surround the religion of Christianity, of which there are thousands.

A recent example of how a contact event spawns a community of belief, and how institutions monitor belief, is the American-based religion of the Nation of Islam. One of the Nation's early leaders was Elijah Robert Poole, who adopted the name Elijah Muhammad. Poole believed that UFOs would come to Earth and bring salvation to his community of believers and punish others who were not believers. The US government was interested in Poole and his followers, and the FBI established a file on him and his community. Within the history of many traditional religions, institutions, including governments, have been involved in monitoring and often forming and shaping the interpretations of the contact event. This fact is becoming less controversial and suggestive of conspiracy to UFO believers, and the focus is shifting now to *how* institutions monitor, and sometimes actively shape, the interpretations of contact events. Perceived contacts with nonhuman intelligences are powerful events with unpredictable social effects.

THE CREATION OF BELIEF AND PRACTICES: A TENUOUS RELATIONSHIP TO THE CONTACT EVENT

In analyzing the contact event and the subsequent interpretations of it, one needs to keep a few things in mind. First, a contact event is not automatically a religious event, and the spotting of an unidentified aerial object is not automatically a UFO event. These experiences become religious events, or UFO events, through an interpretive process.[13] The interpretative process goes through stages of shaping and sometimes active intervention before it is solidified as a religious event, a UFO event, or both. The various types of belief in UFOs can be traced as cultural processes that develop both

spontaneously and intentionally within layers of popular culture and through purposive institutional involvement.

TECHNOLOGY AND NEW FORMS OF RELIGIOUS BELIEF

Scholars of religion were not the first to suggest that the flying
saucer was the symbol of a new, global belief system. Carl
Jung announced it in his little book, published in the 1950s,
Flying Saucers: A Modern Myth of Things Seen in the Skies.
Writing in the late 1960s, Jacques Vallee argued, in *Passport
to Magonia,* that similar patterns could be observed in folklore, religious traditions, and modern UFO events. Scholars
of the history of the flying saucer usually date its emergence
to the beginning of the Cold War and pilot Kenneth Arnold's
sighting of nine, flat, saucerlike discs over Mount Rainier in
1947. Vallee argues, however, that the phenomenon has been
around for thousands of years, perhaps more. He is right. Yet
the ubiquitous cultural framework for understanding them
as the modern UFO did indeed begin around 1947.

Since the 1960s, scholars of religion have made significant progress in identifying the mechanisms of religious
belief, including how social infrastructures inspire new religious movements. Interpretation of UFOs as connected
to religion or religious traditions constitutes a significant
cultural development. New religious movements such as
the Nation of Islam, Scientology, and Jediism incorporate the UFO narrative into older religious traditions and
scriptures.[14] Popular television programs like *Ancient Aliens*
provide viewers with interpretive strategies that encourage
them to view religious visions of the past through the lens

of the modern UFO narrative, turning medieval angels into aliens, for example. What was once a belief localized within small pockets or groups of believers under the umbrella term "UFO religions" is now a widespread worldview that is supercharged by the digital infrastructure that spreads messages and beliefs "virally." The infrastructure of technology has spawned new forms of religion and religiosity, and belief in UFOs has emerged as one such new form of religious belief.

REAL OR IMAGINARY?

The media's representation of the phenomenon often adds some violence to the original event that motivated the belief. Some may understandably ask, "Is it real, or is it imaginary?" It is important to remember that the events themselves pale in comparison to the reality of the social effects. This is a shame. The closer one gets to those engaged in the study of the phenomenon, the more one begins to fathom the complex nature of these events that come to be interpreted as religious, mystical, sacred, or pertaining to UFOs, and the deep commitments of the people who experience them. Each of the scientists with whom I engaged was passionately obsessed with his research, but none of them would ever offer conclusions as to what the phenomenon was or where it came from. The suggestion that the phenomenon is the basis for a new form of religion elicited sneers and disgust. To them, the phenomenon was too sacred to become religious dogma.

It was also, in their opinion, too sacred to be entrusted to the media. Because of my dual research focus, on occasion

I became a reluctant bridge between the scientists and media professionals. On one occasion a videographer, working for a well-known production company, contacted one of the scientists and asked him for a two-sentence quote. At first the scientist was confused, wondering how the videographer had acquired his contact information. He then correctly traced it back to me. In a phone call to me he registered his disgust.

"There is a lot of arrogance in the assumption that I am supposed to condense twenty years of research into the most profound topic in human history into a two-sentence sound bite to be broadcast out to the public so they can consume it with their TV dinner. No thanks," he said.

Interchanges like this, which I witnessed often, reveal the chasm between those engaged in studying the phenomenon and the media representations of it. Ironically, however, it is precisely media representations that create and sustain UFO belief. Is it real, or is it imaginary? What follows suggests that it is both.

THE INVISIBLE TYLER D.

The first rule of Fight Club is . . .
— CHUCK PALAHNIUK, *Fight Club* (1996)

A JOURNEY TO THE DESERT

"You need to wear the blindfold."

Tyler's voice was calm but firm. His southern accent took a bit of the hard edge off the statement, but James and I got the message. It was time to put on our blindfolds. This was one of the conditions to which we had agreed. We were to wear a blindfold for the last forty minutes of the car ride, so we wouldn't be able to see where we were or how we arrived. I had come to call the destination, somewhat tongue-in-cheek, "the sacred place." It was *not* Area 51, I was told. But it *was* a place in New Mexico under a no-fly zone, and it was supposedly a location where one could find artifacts of an extraterrestrial aerial craft that had crashed in 1947. As a professor of religious studies, this was outside my usual research territory, but not by much. The study of religion can get pretty weird.

I called this the sacred place because it marked the location where it is believed that nonhuman intelligence revealed itself to humans. In my field the word that describes this kind of event is *hierophany*. A hierophany is a manifestation of the sacred. It occurs when a nonhuman intelligent being descends from the sky to the ground or otherwise reveals itself. The burning bush that Moses witnessed on Mt. Sinai, as recorded in the Bible, is a classic example of a hierophany. Locations like Roswell, New Mexico, function as sacred places, or sites of hierophanies, to millions of people who believe in extraterrestrials. It is a destination that also happens to be teeming with kitschy shops where tourists and pilgrims can purchase UFO memorabilia. There is a museum that is dedicated to the topic of UFOs, restaurants serve UFO-themed food, and the town hosts an annual four-day UFO festival.

A carnival-like atmosphere is common to many sacred pilgrimage sites. A similar atmosphere can be found in the town of Lourdes, France. In 1858, according to Catholics, the Blessed Virgin Mary appeared to a young girl, Bernadette, and a spring of water miraculously flowed from the ground. Today millions of people journey to the spring at Lourdes to buy water, statues, and other sacred memorabilia. One can purchase Virgin Mary–themed food and drinks, as well as books and pamphlets describing the events of the miracle. Where hierophanies appear, consumerism often follows.

To be clear, to suggest that the location to which we were headed in New Mexico functioned as the site of a hierophany is an interpretation. It is my interpretation. The site held no sacred value for me, although this has changed. My intention was to document how this site in New Mexico functioned as a sacred site for others, particularly the two scientists with whom I was traveling. My research partner was James Master, one of the world's leading scientists and a professor at a major research university. For him, our destination was a place where a nonhuman aerial craft had potentially landed. If artifacts could be found, he believed he could show this had truly happened. Tyler, our host, shared his belief. Tyler believed that this was one of the most significant locations in the history of humanity, and he explained that only a handful of people had been there. I was more interested in observing how James and Tyler, two of the most intelligent and successful people I had ever met, understood the event and the artifacts than in whether the artifacts were, in fact, of nonhuman origin. At this point in the story, that was my position. For Tyler and James, this was a momentous occasion that was also, perhaps ironically, marked by the appearance of a giant, gleaming rainbow in the sky, as I pointed out to my distracted partners.

"Wow!" Tyler said as he glimpsed the rainbow. He looked over at me suspiciously, as if I had somehow conjured it.

James and I fitted the blindfolds over our eyes, an awkward moment for all three of us, or so I thought. Later I learned (because he showed me the pictures) that Tyler had photographed me and James in our blindfolds. He started the car, and we jolted forward. I was riding in the front passenger seat, and as Tyler drove we all rocked to and fro, back and forth, over what had to be a gravel road. We drove for forty minutes and joked about various things, none of which had to do with the reason for our journey. I was nervous, mostly because I couldn't see where I was going. But I was also nervous because I could feel the expectation in the air. James was dying to get his hands on any potential artifacts— the alleged pieces of crashed craft—to study them, and Tyler was almost giddy that he was bringing two people to the site who might help shed light on what he believed was advanced technology that could potentially help humans in significant ways, through either bio- or aerial technologies. I had made it clear that I wasn't going there to ascertain the truth of the event. I was going there to document the belief in extraterrestrial intelligence and the alleged artifacts.

Tyler had told James and me to wear sturdy leather boots to protect our legs from rattlesnakes. The weather would be extreme—the sun would be hot and we might get sunburned, yet the wind chill required us to wear winter jackets. When we arrived at our destination and took off the blindfolds, I looked around and laughed at our appearance. James and I looked ridiculous in puffy jackets, tall leather boots, and cowboy hats. Tyler, though, was dressed stylishly in a jean jacket and short boots. He explained that his body temperature was naturally very warm.

After we had recovered from the trip and sipped some water, Tyler configured two metal detectors and showed us a map of where the craft had landed. He said that, when the crash occurred in 1947, the government had taken the craft, hidden it away in a secret place, and disguised the area with tin cans and debris to prevent others from finding any remaining artifacts. In fact, looking around, the area was covered over with tons of tin cans. The cans were rusty and most of them had disintegrated into a powdery rubble that resembled compost. He further explained that our metal detectors were special and had been configured to identify the artifacts. He paused and surveyed the area. It was a beautiful day with few clouds. The wind whistled past us, and all was silent except for its sound. We stood and looked around. There were tumbleweeds, rocks, and the rust-colored cans strewn as far as I could see. The landscape was eerie yet beautiful. I was drawn to one place in particular, as it looked familiar to me. It was a small mesa. Tyler noticed that I had looked in that direction several times.

"Do you recognize that area?"

"What?" I wasn't sure where he was going with the question. He knew I'd never been there.

"This scene was probably recreated in the first episode of the last season of *The X-Files*," he said.

James and I stood there looking at him, incredulous.

"Yes," he continued. "Someone from their production team had either been here or knew someone who had. It makes me wonder if they had an insider on their team."

What was already a weird occasion just got weirder. I let Tyler's statement sink in slowly. He had just said that the supposed site of a real extraterrestrial craft crash landing, where I currently stood, was featured in the opening episode of the last season of *The X-Files*. I silently scoffed. His statement sounded more ridiculous than James and I looked at that moment. I looked at the mesa again. It did look like the scene from the television show.

It took a moment as my thoughts sped through several different steps and scenarios in an attempt to process Tyler's statement. It was data, and I felt that I shouldn't reject it outright. It was then that I felt the click of realization. This was not so surprising after all. Of course this place was mythologized in one of the most popular television shows in history. Of course it would be taken up, interpreted, and spun, and then projected to millions, perhaps even billions, of people through the various screens of television, film, computer, and phone. It was only now that I felt the momentousness of the occasion. My belief in the objective truth of this site didn't matter. It had already become true for millions of people, through media. Tyler and James were right. This place was a big deal. I was standing on ground zero of the new religion.

CODES OF SILENCE, THE INVISIBLES, AND THE INVITATION TO THE SITE

Throughout the day, James and I took opportunities to compare notes. Was Tyler setting us up? If so, for what reason? Were we pawns in a covert plot to disseminate disinformation? The answers to these questions didn't matter to me. They didn't matter because I wasn't there to determine the truth behind the artifacts, but to observe the formation of belief in the artifacts and to track the various directions this belief took. In the history of religions, there are always artifacts: the Ark of the Covenant, Noah's Ark, the Shroud of Turin. The artifacts are important to believers, and they are controversial for nonbelievers. They spawn religious communities and, ironically, fictional portrayals. If we were there as pawns of a disinformation campaign, I thought, this revealed that powerful interest groups were still heavily involved in the creation of UFO/extraterrestrial belief—a fact that has already been well established.[1] I was open to that possibility and would not have been at all surprised if it were true now.

Jesus's presence and message were given many different interpretations by early Christians, and they didn't all agree. In fact, they often vehemently disagreed with one another. Almost four hundred years after Jesus was killed by the Roman government, that very government decreed Christianity to be a state religion, and they put their might behind one interpretation and deemed it universal. Other interpretations became heretical, and those who advocated for them were sometimes punished with ridicule—or worse.

In this respect, the UFO/extraterrestrial belief system was no different: its message had been managed. However, I was curious to observe how the site and the artifacts informed and influenced the belief systems of my research partners, two scientists who were at the top of their games, the pinnacle of their careers. Each had a reputation built on revolutionary innovation and discoveries that pushed the boundaries of the possible. Their technologies were cultural game changers—there was no other way to put it. My quest was to understand how their beliefs informed the creation of their technologies and contributed to a larger UFO myth and narrative.

James and Tyler believed they had evidence, not just faith, to support their belief in the extraterrestrial source of the artifacts and the authenticity of the crash site. Prior to this trip, Tyler had given James an analysis of some of the parts. James knew what he was looking at, and, according to him, if this analysis actually corresponded to the makeup of the artifacts, then they were one of two things: they were something that someone paid millions, if not billions, of dollars to fabricate or "something" made them somewhere other than on Earth with technologies we did not understand.

At one point during the day James looked at me and asked, "Why would someone do that? Spend millions of dollars to create these parts, and then just throw them here in the desert in hope that we would find it? It just doesn't make sense."

James's track record as a scientist was impeccable, and in part my quest was motivated by the desire to understand the connections between his belief and his skills. He is one of the leading scientists in the world, and he had the instruments and the technical skill to determine whether the artifacts were genuinely anomalous. He was eager to locate some of them, if any remained.

How he and I came to travel to the site was an odd story. A few months prior to our trip, I had organized a small conference, to which Tyler had not been invited, on the phenomenon. The small, closed meeting was unique because it brought together ufologists and scientists with scholars of the humanities, all of whom studied the phenomenon. The goal of the conference was to compare notes and learn new things from people whose fields were different from our own. We assumed that the things we would learn would include new data. The most important lesson we learned, however, was that the codes of conduct that govern academic scholarship are very different from the codes that govern the behavior of those who study the phenomenon in an official capacity. This realization was eye-opening for me and would determine the scope—and limits—of my research.

The code of conduct for academics demands transparency. We reveal our sources as a matter of practice and ethics. It is an ethical imperative that guides our work. I found out that the code of conduct for half of the conference attendees was exactly the opposite, and for very good reasons. Scientist-ufologists are vetted extensively before their employment in the field and, once hired, take oaths to keep their sources secret. The code of confidentiality extends throughout the communities of people associated with the government who work in specific areas of space research and particularly in the field concerned with unidentified aerial objects. The one thing that you are not allowed to discuss, if you are employed in this capacity, is the very thing you study. They maintain their silence for important reasons, one of which is national security. Due to our different codes of ethics, the interface between the academics and the other researchers at the conference was fraught with tension. I learned that I needed to take my new research partners' ethical codes seriously and respect their silences and their confidentialities. If I didn't, I could get some people in a lot of trouble. This realization hit home when, at the conference, I witnessed a breach in the code of silence.

During one of the sessions an attendee stood up and interrupted a speaker. In the closed academic meetings in which I had participated, this was not typical behavior. Members of the audience, including me, were shocked. The usual protocol dictated that attendees wait until a speaker is finished and then ask questions. I touched the attendee on the shoulder and asked him to wait. He refused, politely. The professor tried to continue, but the attendee lost his polite demeanor and loudly proclaimed that the professor who was speaking had no authority to report his findings. The two men began to vehemently disagree with one another. Dismayed at the noncollegial nature of the interchange, I quickly called for a coffee break while the two continued to argue. As attendees filed out the door for coffee, the two men moved toward me. From snippets of their conversation I understood that they had both been aware of a research study that was apparently not public, but secret. Each had taken an oath to not reveal the findings from the study, but none of us in the audience knew anything about it. During the break I spoke to several attendees and none of the academics understood what had happened. They were so unaware of the code of silence that the others had to observe—it was so far removed from their own fields and ethical codes—that the small spat may as well not even have happened. For me, it was just the beginning of an education about the lives of people who study the phenomenon from the inside, the invisibles—people whose names are washed from the internet on a regular basis. Their merits and accomplishments are never to be known. They are, literally, removed from history as if they never existed.

On the day after I got back from the conference, I received a phone call from Tyler. Now that I had begun to understand a little more about the phenomenon, he would like to take me to a special place in New Mexico where I might understand a little more about the phenomenon's physical nature. The timing of his invitation was odd, and I wondered if he was somehow aware of what happened at the conference. I was suspicious of him. I told him that I would go to the place in New Mexico if I could take my research partner, James. Tyler said no. He explained that he needed to obtain special permission to take me, and that it was out of the question to take another person. I understood. However, I was not going to go without another person, and James, a scientist who studies the phenomenon, was my choice. Plus, James was an academic, and therefore I understood his framework—transparency—and he understood mine. In a sense, James was familiar and I trusted him. I emailed him and asked if he would go if Tyler consented.

James's reply was instant: "Hell, yes."

We both waited for Tyler to change his mind.

After a few days, I received a note from Tyler. He had warmed to the idea of having James on the adventure. When I told James, he was elated. In the back of my mind I had known that Tyler would want James to go on the trip, because if anyone in the world could analyze a piece of alleged alien crash debris and determine anything about it, it would be him. I knew that Tyler would research James, and he would come to this conclusion. I didn't know it at the time, but Tyler was on a quest to understand the nature of the artifacts, and I was a part of that quest.

MEETING TYLER: VIRTUALLY

I'd put off meeting Tyler even though acquaintances had told me that he wanted to meet me. He was what I call a "meta-experiencer." When I started my research in January 2012, I thought that the people I would interview and learn about would be experiencers, people who believed they either saw unidentified aerial phenomena or had contact, in some way, with their inhabitants. I quickly learned that experiencers attracted people other than just those like me who were interested in learning about their experiences and beliefs. They also attracted scientists. The scientists were interested in what the experiencers saw and how they saw it, and often applied this information to their own work. I coined the term "meta-experiencers" to describe this group of scientists. I cautiously observed them, noting that most were reticent to admit they believed in the reality of UFOs, but they readily scooped data from the primary experiencers. Tyler was one such person, an employee in the space industry.

I was suspicious of Tyler because he was different from most of the other meta-experiencers. For one thing, he was very wealthy. I'd heard that he traveled in a private jet. He drove an expensive sports car. He was rumored to be an MMA, or mixed martial arts, fighter, and to have competed in several publicized fights. Yet it wasn't his wealth or his hobbies that caused me to be suspicious. It was his affiliations. There were other rumors that he had worked for several government agencies. I avoided him because of these rumors. I knew from previous scholars' work that when one scratched the surface of the topic of UFO events, eventually one would find that governments were also interested in the topic, and one might cross paths with agents.[2] The thought of government agents wanting to meet me was disturbing, mostly because of what I'd seen on television, which, granted, was based on stereotypes. I was happy, however, to carry on a correspondence over email, but even that was different from the typical email correspondence.

My first communication from Tyler that was not part of an email thread directed to several recipients was a text message. It was the longest text message I had ever received, full of information about how he came to study the phenomenon. He sent videos of where he worked in New Mexico, Florida, and other places. He also sent videos of his conversations with friends. These were very odd. His friends never looked at the camera, and they spoke as if they were unaware that they were being filmed. I quickly surmised that, in fact, they did not know. Tyler was outfitted with various types of cameras hidden in his clothes, disguised, and strategically placed on his body, and was recording everything. I knew that if and when I finally did meet him, he would be videotaping me too. That, among other things, was a deterrent.

Yet, Tyler's personal history was compelling. Through our correspondence I learned that since the age of eighteen he had worked for the US space program, first as an intern and then as an engineer for the space shuttle program. He worked on almost every space shuttle that was ever launched, and he spoke about each as if it were a living thing. He described how each shuttle had its own personality, its own noises and sounds. Tyler's passion was launching rockets and

shuttles and for anything that had to do with space exploration. He sent me videos of his conversations with several
astronauts, just casual conversations. I wondered how they
would feel knowing that I, a stranger to them, was watching
them have lunch with their friend Tyler while I was sitting
in my office at work. I found it amusing, and fascinating.
Tyler's circle of colleagues consisted of generals, scientists,
and astronauts. He had another set of colleagues—surgeons
and venture capitalists—and he began to share more of his
life in this sector. I was confused by his breadth of knowledge
and skills; on the one hand, he was an aeronautical engineer,
and on the other hand, he was a biomedical entrepreneur. He
was a wealthy rocket scientist. It all just didn't seem to add
up. One day I asked him to explain the connections between
his diverse fields of expertise.

Through a combination of videos, text messages, and
emails, Tyler explained that part of his mission was to translate the information he learned from space exploration into
biomedical technologies. One video featured the CEO of one
of Tyler's companies in Tampa praising him. In one scene,
the CEO stood in front of a promotional video for a biomedical project. The video featured a photo of Tyler in a blue
flight uniform, wearing aviator sunglasses, posed in front of
a giant rocket. Tyler worked with venture capitalists and with
surgeons and medical researchers to implement his visions.
He explained that he owns more than forty patents, and that
he mostly works from home, on his deck, in the sun.

"I get paid to think. And to match up experts who can
implement my vision."

I asked him why he was interested in carrying on a
correspondence with me, a scholar of religion. He said, "I
have mentors in the space program. One of them, who is

now retired, explained that the next discovery in my field is going to come from your field. I am at the limit of understanding what I can from a materialist perspective. My mentor explained that mysticism, religion, and consciousness is where I need to go to learn what's next. That the mind–machine interface is the next frontier."

Tyler's career had been going full speed ahead until the death of one of his mentors and friends, the brilliant astronaut Judith Resnik, who was killed when the space shuttle *Challenger* exploded in 1986. He recalled this disaster and its effect on him in a video he sent to me while he was on business in Cape Canaveral. In the video, he was standing on concrete slabs at the Air Force base. He was there to pay his respects to the *Challenger*'s crew, and to his friend Judy.

"This is the burial ground of the *Challenger*. Pretty sad, huh? The shuttle is buried here, in chunks of concrete."

I hadn't known that this was the ultimate destination of the *Challenger*. Tyler went on to explain more about that day.

"Her last hug showed me that on some level she must have known. Anyway, for us on the ground, we were looking up as it launched. We were all excited as this mission had received so much publicity, and the president was watching it too. On that day, we all huddled in a group and stared at the capsule as she left Earth. She soared higher and higher, and we squinted to keep her in focus. Then, well . . . yeah. We saw the explosion. I instantly felt a shock of pain in my stomach. I knew immediately what happened. Everyone else was in denial. They refused to see it. I don't blame them. Those were our friends. I saw the sparks and the debris start to fall. I could feel my heart and my spirit—they just died. No feeling left, just a gaping hole. I left the group and went down and looked out at the ocean. My spirit and soul called out to my friend Judy. 'I'm sorry.' That is what I wanted to say to her. I watched the wisps of debris floating into the ocean, and I knew I was never going to be the same."

Tyler's voice, now strained and broken, trailed off in the video, but he was still filming. I could still see the concrete chunks. I watched the video in silence. Tyler was still recording, but he couldn't speak. I sat and watched quietly. I can still picture myself, sitting in my office chair, watching. I will not forget that day. Until then, I had been mostly amused by Tyler. This video put an end to that feeling. His sad story revealed itself to me, at that moment, in its greatness, its largeness. Tyler's story was bigger than Tyler. It was also part of American history. Yet, Tyler's part in this history would never be known. Was Tyler obsessed with recording videos because his story was erased, and had to be erased? I didn't know. Probably. The video marked a turning point in my estimation of who Tyler was and what he had contributed, and was contributing, to a history that, ironically, was unknown.

Later he spoke to me about the aftermath of the *Challenger* disaster.

"Like a lot of astronauts and people in the program, I dedicated my life to the program and its success. That means that I didn't have a personal life. It took its toll. Right after the *Challenger* accident my wife wanted a divorce. That, and the loss of my friend Judy, put me over the edge. I developed heart palpitations that landed me in the hospital for a few days, but things all went better with some medication that I took for a few months . . . but it was a rough time. I was very depressed and struggling through life and had no idea of anything about the phenomenon. In fact, I was a pure skeptic and didn't believe in anything in that realm.

"Someone left a book in my office at work, which had no title on the black cover. It ended up in my briefcase one day, and I took it out and started reading it. It was Carl Sagan's book on the cosmos and space travel. It was completely different from anything at my day job launching space shuttles. I noticed as I read the book that I was able to settle down and even sleep well. It became my saving grace, and I read it every night. His views of the universe expanded my knowledge and put all my problems in perspective. It was my turning point, and I knew that there was either existing or soon to exist technology that was much further advanced than the space shuttle that could allow for interstellar and superluminal space travel. A few months later I started work in a very special facility at the space center, which was the next step, I think, in my evolution to off-planet experiences."

Tyler's personal crisis after the *Challenger* disaster led him to his discovery of the phenomenon. As he grieved the loss of Judy and the crew, as well as his divorce, he knew that he couldn't go on working in the program. The realization hit him hard, as his own identity was fused with the program and space exploration. He explained that one day, as he contemplated his departure from the program, a general entered his office and issued a request for proposals for experiments to be run on the space shuttle *Columbia*. As the general spoke, Tyler said, "I had a memory, and it was about this experiment. I knew it would work. It was to test whether or not a noncharged material could speak with a charged material. This could only be tested in a nongravity environment. Don't ask me how I knew this would work; I just did." The general, however, didn't think the experiment would work. Tyler did not have a PhD, which was required to run the experiment.

"As much as the memory of that idea was there as a reality to me, so was the will to get the general to say yes to this experiment. Basically, he thought it was stupid, and so did everyone else. But I did get a professor to agree to help me with the experiment, even though he thought it wouldn't work. He wanted to publish the results and to have run an experiment on the space shuttle, and to him, whether it worked or not didn't matter. It was the publication that mattered."

The general reluctantly agreed to the experiment, and to everyone's surprise, it worked. Tyler explained what happened afterward, which marked the turning point in his career.

"A few days after the experiment worked, me and the professor were called to Washington, DC. I was excited, as I thought that I would get an award. Instead, we were asked to go into the basement, which, by the way, is never good. We went in, and we all sat down—me, the professor, a few people who had witnessed the experiment, and some guards. After a few minutes the door opened and a two-star general entered the room. We all stood.

"He barked out, 'Who the hell came up with this idea?'

"I immediately stiffened with shock. The professor pointed at me. 'He did.'

"At that point I knew I wasn't getting an award. Instead, I was interrogated.

"'Where did you get that idea?' the general yelled at me.

"I could only tell him the truth, that it was a memory. That sounded like bullshit, but it was the truth. The professor confirmed it. Once the general was satisfied that I was probably an idiot, he sent me out of the room. The next week at work, I was given a plaque, a patent, and five hundred dollars. I decided that week to quit my job and go into business with a surgeon buddy of mine. I decided to take my 'memory' and use it for good."

At this point Tyler and his associates went into business pursuing the biomedical applications of his ideas, or memories. He was successful. He wrote patent after patent, and sold his first biomedical company to a public corporation for an undisclosed amount of money. It provided him with enough money to retire, which he did, but his retirement proved to be brief.

"After a few months, I was bored. I knew I had to go back into the space program. It was my core passion. As if on cue, as I was passing through an airport, two men approached me and handed me a card. They asked me if I wanted to come back to the program, and on the card was a phone number. They told me to call it, so I did. I know that sounds like it is straight out of a movie, but that's what happened."

When Tyler returned to the program, things had changed. He explained that he was now connected to a source that he believed was part of an off-planet intelligence. He felt that it had been with him since a few months after he saw the *Challenger* explode.

"After the disaster I started working in a very special facility at the space center. It was the next step in my evolution of my knowledge of off-planet phenomenon."

What he learned there wasn't typical information. He wasn't shown anything and didn't read about anything, but he believes he was in the proximity of something that emitted energy and frequencies that changed the way he thought. His desk was next to a square room that was covered in concrete and metal.

"There was something in there that either emitted frequencies or signals and they didn't want those to escape or they didn't want signals to get in. I never knew which. It was a mysterious place, and we weren't allowed to talk about it."

That room, Tyler felt, zapped him with energy that changed the "frequencies" of his body and his thoughts. It was after this experience that he began to have more "memories" of biomedical technologies.

"In the program, I started to find myself on jobs where I interfaced directly with the phenomenon. I know its language. It does speak to us, in space. I don't know who is responsible for putting me on these jobs. I think that somehow *they* are responsible for it. My own direct boss doesn't know what I do. This is how the program works."

Tyler explained that his connection to off-planet intelligence helps him create biotechnologies. The technologies he has created seem to me as if they originated in an episode of *Star Wars* or *Star Trek*. One of the applications of his inspiration is a material that has been etched at the molecular level with information. The etching codes the material with information that human bone "reads" as itself. It is then incorporated into diseased human tissue and bone, which helps the body recuperate from cancer and other illnesses. Tyler showed me a picture of one of the patients who was healed through this treatment. Jane is a radiant young mother of twins. She had bone cancer and was told that she would never walk again. Tyler sent me a picture of a thank you card she had written to him, noting that she had believed she would never walk again, let alone care for her young boys, and now she was doing both.

At this point, my curiosity was piqued. Tyler, his life, and his current pursuits intrigued me. I decided to meet him. If he was an agent, he certainly was an accomplished and productive one, and I didn't feel as if I was in danger.

He had shared information about his family, so I knew he was a family man as well. Additionally, as he and I continued our correspondence, I had uncovered a lot more historical information about the beginnings of the Russian and the American space programs. This information helped me contextualize Tyler's place within these institutions.

Many of the scientists and astronauts who work for the space programs most likely do not believe in extraterrestrial intelligence, or that humans are in contact with that intelligence, but the founders of both the Russian and the American space programs did. Konstantin Tsiolkovsky, regarded as the founding father of rocketry and aeronautics, believed that ethereal beings, or nonhuman intelligences, were trying to communicate with humans through symbols. He wrote:

> We are made as the "ethereal beings," existing beyond our dimensions of recognized reality. These higher beings are in communication with us, reading our thoughts and sending us messages through celestial symbols which most of us do not even perceive, much less understand. A genius is one who comprehends and channels these messages from higher beings into technologies, products, and even art.[3]

Tsiolkovsky perhaps regarded himself as one of these geniuses, as he discovered the equations that would later help scientists develop rockets to take humans off Earth and into space.

The American space program had its own version of Tsiolkovsky. Jack Parsons was uniquely American in that he collaborated with Aleister Crowley and L. Ron Hubbard and spent time both launching rockets and engaging in provocative rituals in the Los Angeles desert. He also believed that he was in contact with extraterrestrial intelligences. He launched his experiments on days that were ritually significant to him, such as Halloween, and his prelaunch rituals paid homage to the intelligences with whom he believed himself to be in contact. His life ended tragically. He was thirty-seven when one of his rockets exploded as he was experimenting in his garage, and he perished with it. A few months after his death, there was a very public sighting of UFOs over the White House. Parsons's widow and friends attributed this sighting to his death.[4]

In keeping with the code of silence that permeates the industry, most of the astronauts and NASA employees I interviewed didn't know about this history, or if they did, they didn't want to talk about it. The mere mention of it embarrassed them. When I asked Tyler what he thought of Jack Parsons and Tsiolkovsky, he expressed admiration for their genius but was genuinely shocked and surprised when I described what they believed and their rituals. I had begun to understand Tyler as being part of a lineage of people like Tsiolkovsky and Parsons—people who believed that they were in contact with nonhuman intelligences and believed that those intelligences were directing their paths and seeding them with information that directly led to the creation of innovative technologies. Whereas the former men focused on aeronautics, Tyler had a dual focus—aeronautics and biotechnologies. I also began to understand Tyler as a contemporary version of the famed Colonel Philip Corso.

Colonel Corso was a military man who claimed to be an agent whose task was to seed private industry with crashed extraterrestrial craft under the guise of Russian or Chinese technology. The hope was that private industry would reverse-engineer the technology and provide Americans with an edge in the global marketplace. His book, *The Day After Roswell* (1997), appeared on the *New York Times* best-seller list. The book fueled a modern version of the myth of Prometheus—the notion that nonhuman, advanced intelligences (gods, even) provided humans with advanced technology. But it also fueled a conspiracy theory that simultaneously explained the origins of modern technology and accused the government of covering up the secret of extraterrestrial life.

Significantly, technology has often been described using the language of the supernatural. Computer programmers are "wizards," and "devils" in computers assist users with techno-logical tasks. Social media can and will "read your mind."[5] A much-quoted statement by Arthur C. Clarke, that "any sufficiently advanced technology is indistinguishable from magic," solidifies a division between technology and magic while also establishing their connection.[6] The assumption is that if we were sufficiently advanced, we would understand that something that appears magical, such as an advanced propulsion spacecraft, is not magical at all but technological. But something far stranger and more complex was at work here, as reflected in the lives of the founders of the space programs and in the work of the new, contemporary version of Colonel Corso, Tyler D. It was a fusion of magic, or the supernatural, and the technological. And somehow silence was the key to understanding this connection. Whereas the original Colonel Corso functioned as a contemporary Prometheus and was punished in the public court of ridicule, the contemporary Corso, Tyler D., worked silently, invisibly. His invisibility ensured his success and was somehow a key to it.[7]

MEETING TYLER: IN PERSON

At this point, my expectations of Tyler were running very high, and he did not disappoint me. We arranged to meet in Atlanta at the annual conference for my discipline, the American Academy of Religion. Even though I was sold on Tyler's legitimate place in the space program, I was still suspicious of him, mostly because I knew he would be outfitted with cameras, but also because I was still unsure exactly what he did and why he was interested in meeting me. I convinced one of my colleagues, Jeff Kripal, to accompany me to the meeting. Jeff's work on religion had helped me understand the research direction upon which I had embarked, and I hoped to rely on his input and assessment of Tyler and his occupations. I had primed Jeff for the meeting, telling him of my concerns. I also knew an experiencer who knew Tyler. His interpretation of Tyler was informed by his belief in extraterrestrials and his Christian beliefs, so I wasn't that surprised when he told me that Tyler was probably an angel, which to him meant that he was a person who is part human and part extraterrestrial.

"You are just about to meet someone who is not human," he said. "He is older than both of us, but he looks twenty years younger. I don't know what he is."

We were to meet at a restaurant near the conference, but it was jam-packed with scholars of religion. The wait for a table was over an hour. Jeff and I decided to wait at the bar for Tyler. I was nervous, and Jeff picked up on my unease. We laughed. Soon a tall, thin man with thick brown hair appeared at the restaurant window and peered in. It was Tyler. The window was mirrored glass on the outside, and as I turned I looked directly into his eyes as he combed his hair and checked his appearance. He couldn't see me. He then walked in and recognized us immediately. I noticed the details of his clothes. He was extremely well dressed in a classic suit and a dress shirt with cuff links. Gucci. His attire and demeanor distinguished him from the scholars of religion, who were mostly disheveled and were milling about and eating lunch. He introduced himself, and we shook hands. I couldn't tell how old he was, maybe in his late forties or early fifties, but he did look extremely fit and youthful, just as the experiencer had said. Upon learning about the wait for lunch, he immediately called his hotel, the Ritz, and secured a table for us there.

Tyler turned out to be very charismatic in person, just as he was virtually. He laughed easily and was as comfortable talking about his family as he was talking about science. His natural charm impressed Jeff, who invited him to his house in Houston for dinner to meet his wife and family. I had hoped Jeff would be a little reserved and keep Tyler at arm's distance, but Tyler's charisma proved too powerful and was no match for my suggestion that perhaps Tyler was using it for a purpose. None of my warnings were heeded. This would be just the first case where Tyler's charm and social abilities were in evidence. Every person or group of people to whom I introduced him was taken by his demeanor. He was some kind of rock star, and that just added to my suspicion of him.

TYLER'S PROTOCOL

At lunch Tyler explained that he had a specific protocol for connecting with off-planet intelligence. It was a physical and mental protocol, and as Tyler explained the details of it, Jeff and I nodded in recognition. Many religious traditions advocate a physical protocol, like yoga, meditation, or contemplation, that involves the body and the mind. These traditions, it is believed, help practitioners connect with the sacred. Tyler's description of his own protocol reminded us of religious practitioners and these traditions.

"I basically believe, and there is evidence for this, that our DNA is a receptor and transmitter. It works at a certain frequency—the same frequency, in fact, that we use to communicate with our satellites in deep space. Humans are a type of satellite, in fact. So, in order to receive the signals and to transmit the signals, we have to tune our physical bodies and DNA. Because of this, I make sure I sleep really well. I use the eight plus one rule. That is, I sleep for eight hours, wake up, and then make myself go back to bed for an hour. That one hour, the top-off, really makes or breaks my day. I barely drink alcohol, as it interferes with sleep, and I never drink coffee. Coffee really messes up the signal."

I listened to Tyler as I sipped from my coffee cup, trying to fight the exhaustion that comes from cramming too many activities into a three-day conference. Jeff and I took turns asking Tyler more questions about his protocol and his connection to the off-planet intelligence.

"How does this help with your connection, and what does that connection feel like?" I asked.

"I also have to be in the sun. So I wake up, and the previous night I will have gone to bed a little dehydrated. Then, I get my extra hour of sleep and go out into the sun. While I bask in the light of vitamin D, I drink a tall glass of water, which flushes my cells and rehydrates them. This is better than coffee. It is at this point that I can usually feel the connection. I know I've established connection when the thoughts that show up in my mind don't seem like my own. They are unfamiliar. With practice you can feel the difference."

"So, you recognize these thoughts as different from your own?" Jeff asked.

"Yes, but you also have to understand that the environment also 'wakes up' and validates that they are speaking to you. See? I can explain it this way. I get a thought, and it comes out of nowhere. It comes with a certain feeling, like a hit. Then, usually within a few hours, something will happen that will validate that it was them, and that I should act on it. Here's an example.

"A key event of my life happened because of an errant email. I was sending a note to a friend and accidently sent it to the wrong 'John,' who was a former neighbor from years ago. The wrong John read my email thinking I was asking him to work with me to fly an experiment on the NASA KC-135 vomit comet about capacitors, so he developed a one-page concept and sent it back to me. I was like, *who is this and why is he sending this to me?* I didn't know anything about pacemakers or capacitors, nor did I email him my thoughts, which I had had earlier that day. Well, long story short, he emailed me back and said it must have been an errant email from me and from there we kicked off a new project and flew it, and he used that data and knowledge at his company to develop a longer-lasting capacitor for pacemakers! What's more, what I learned from him about pacemaker capacitors in that process helped me understand and connect some dots on how some OP [Off Planet] craft operate, given they use a highly charged capacitor of sorts in their electrogravitic machine."

"So you're talking about synchronicities or coincidences?" I asked.

"Maybe. In order to make the right call, you have to be in tune with your environment, and tune your DNA to receive the signal, and then pay attention. Be on the lookout for the confirmations, and then act on it."

The "accidental" aspect of Tyler's protocol brought to my mind the biochemist Kary Mullis, who had discovered the highly influential polymerase chain reaction and won the Nobel Prize for the discovery in 1993. He also had an anomalous experience that he referred to as a UFO encounter, although he was very careful not to "conclude" that was what it was. I was struck by Mullis's description of his own process of creativity and its similarity to what Tyler was telling us:

> Creativity is when you are trying to figure something out and something else keeps intruding. You finally give in to it, and it turns out to be the answer you were looking for. Perhaps something is lost and instead of looking for it, you let your hands lead you to it with your eyes closed. You might be looking something up and find the wrong subject and it turns out not only to be related, but to be exactly what you were after. It's not an accident. It was inevitable and it all makes perfect sense after the moment, but it's unexpected. That's how creativity happens. The focused beam of your consciousness is very narrow, but you have a creepy sense of what is right behind you.[8]

Tyler's protocol was similar to what I knew from several researchers within the UFO community. Within many of these communities, the name for this contact is the "download." It describes the process of connection with off-planet entities. Researcher Grant Cameron writes about the download experience and suggests that creativity does not necessarily stem from a high IQ or special talent, but instead comes from the ability to tap into "nonlocal intelligence." He said that he originally intended to write a book about what he called "the disclosure by an alien force that humans are not alone," but instead the focus of the book turned to the process of "the download":

> Many modern musicians are very interested in UFOs and extraterrestrial life. . . . As that book neared a final first draft, the whole focus changed. It became apparent that it was more important to talk about downloads and inspirations. What was happening to musicians became only a small part of the story. Following a lecture on the alien-music connection in Boulder, Colorado, some in the audience maintained that it was the devil and evil forces that were influencing modern music. Somewhat taken aback by this criticism, and the old idea of a battle for men's minds by forces of good and evil, I had to sit back and re-examine my world view. I grew up in a home where my mother was a church organist for four decades. That inspired me to see if the composers of the church hymns experienced the same downloads and inspirations as modern musicians. It turned out that they had. That meant that if the devil was behind downloads and inspirations in rock and roll, it appeared that he had also composed all the church music as well.[9]

Like Tyler, Cameron believes that the intelligence behind the download is nonhuman. He also utilizes the language of quantum mechanics; the theme of nonlocality permeates many discussions of the download and processes of extreme creativity. Heather Berlin, a neurologist at the Icahn School of Medicine at Mount Sinai, offers an analysis of the creative mind that supports the idea that creative individuals experience their innovative ideas as external to themselves, or as supplied by external agents:

> So I think that a lot of what's happening in the brain is happening outside awareness and we—when we have our sort of conscious brain highly active—it's kind, it's kind of suppressing a lot of what's going on outside of oneself. Sometimes when people are being creative they say it almost feels like things are coming from outside of them when they are in this sort of flow state. We're starting to understand a little bit more about that state and it seems to be that when people are being creative in the moment that the part of their brain that has to do with their sense of self, self-awareness, self-consciousness is turned down. It's called the dorso-lateral prefrontal cortex. . . . If you think about it a similar pattern of brain activation happens during dreams or during daydreaming or some types of meditation or hypnosis where you lose your sense of self and time and place. It allows the filter to come off so that novel associations are okay, you know. Dreams don't all make sense. That's where the creativity comes in.[10]

Significantly, Berlin's research might suggest that creativity does not originate from an external source, although some creative subjects like Tyler experience it that way. When I pushed Tyler to explain how his method works, he also resorted to the language of quantum theory.

"Observation makes things real," he said. He paused and looked away, and then continued.

"I don't know why it works. It's more important to me *that* it works. You saw the pictures of Jane. She can walk. She can now care for her kids. I can't spend my time thinking about the *how* of the process; I just use the process because it works. Let me tell you about a room where I work. It is a special room outfitted with the latest technologies. It is a smart room. We put the best scientists and thinkers in the world in the room, and then we just let them think. There is a complete sense of freedom in the room. Nothing that is ever said in the room is laughed at. We could talk about a purple unicorn flying through space on a pickle. No one would laugh. The point is this—that some of the most innovative technologies we have and use come from what goes on in that room. In that room, we dream the impossible, and then we make it possible. See that phone near your coffee cup? I assume you use its technologies?"

Jeff and I looked down at my pink iPhone.

"*That* room?" Jeff asked.

"*That* room," Tyler said.

When lunch ended, Tyler picked up the entire check.

A few weeks after our first in-person meeting, I reached out to Tyler. I sent him a text and asked him how he was doing. He responded back with a picture. It was a picture of a snifter of brandy and a partially smoked cigar.

"Celebrating?" I asked.

His response was, "Yes."

He had sold a company and the money from the shares increased his savings account significantly. It would have been a wonderful day for me, and I would have been celebrating with family and friends. Tyler, however, was alone, in his laboratory, with the artifacts, a cigar, and a snifter of brandy.

BACK IN THE DESERT

Tyler and I heard James yell. He was on top of a small hill and waved for us to come.

"He found a part!" Tyler said.

We walked over to where James was standing. He was examining a small, metallic object. It had been identified as an artifact by the metal detector. At that point, both scientists went into collection mode. Tyler took out a plastic bag and a label. He photographed the specimen and labeled it with the date, and he also photographed where it was found. Then he put it in a special bag he carried for the occasion. We took a moment to process the find. In my mind, I was still entertaining the possibility that the parts were placed here for James and me to find. But James found this particular part lodged in a crevice between a bunch of rocks in a gully that certainly looked to me like a nesting place for rattlesnakes. It potentially had arrived there from a washout of the stream bed area—unearthed after years of laying under detritus. He had reached down through the rocks to get the specimen. Evidently James, who was wearing long leather gloves, was a trooper for the cause. The day was almost over, so if we were to find more parts, we had to look more carefully.

Tyler and I decided to team up to make the process more efficient. He swung the metal detector low to the ground, and I carried the shovel and poked around to try to find any parts that the detector might have missed. Much of what we found was normal metal. As we neared the mesa, Tyler's metal detector started to beep loudly. We both got excited. I came with my shovel, but he had already bent down and picked up a very large specimen. It was a metallic piece like James's.

We yelled to James, and we all looked it over in the sun. Tyler believed this had been a part of the craft's exterior.

At the end of the day, we had found several metallic artifacts. At this point night was falling, and it was getting dark and cold. We headed back to our hotel. Later, at dinner, we discussed our next steps. Tyler warned us that, because the parts were metallic, we could get stopped by airport security, should we carry them back with us. James agreed to take all the parts with him so he could study them. Thinking of being stopped at the airport, I agreed to let James have the items I had found. Besides, what could I possibly do with them?

The day after our foray into the desert was sunny, clear, and beautiful. We were all elated from the proceedings of the previous day. I felt James's excitement and Tyler's sense of accomplishment. James had the specimens and couldn't wait to analyze them. Tyler had brought two scholars to the site—two people with widely divergent skills and methods, who could potentially help him understand what he had. On the long drive to the airport we exchanged many theories. We were all well acquainted with the theories of Jacques Vallee, the famous researcher, astronomer, and computer scientist. Vallee's approach addressed three aspects: the physical aspect, which Tyler represented; the testimonial aspect, represented by experiencers; and the social aspect, how belief in the phenomenon persists regardless of whether there is any verifiable evidence to support it. Whereas Tyler and James represented the first two aspects, I represented the third.

We arrived at the airport, and Tyler sailed right past security, past first class, past economy class, and out the other side. He seemed to be literally beyond the law, whereas James and I were not. James and I walked slowly through the long lines, and we waited to get searched. As we neared the TSA agents, we both became quiet. I made it through the line without incident. James did not.

James had put the artifacts in his carry-on bag. As the bag moved slowly down the conveyor belt and through the X-ray scanner, the whole thing suddenly stopped. The contraption shut down with a loud BEEEP. Everyone scrambled and suddenly James's line was redirected to another scanner. James's bag had to be rerun through the scanner. I looked at my friend and saw the horror on his face. As I exited the line, I found Tyler in an airport cafe, looking for us. He and I sat and watched our friend James's bag going through the scanner again.

"Don't worry," Tyler said to reassure me. "He'll be okay."

The bag re-scan went without further incident. Security searched James, his suitcase, his jacket, and everything that he was carrying. By the time he made it through to where Tyler and I were standing, sweat drops glittered on his face and forehead.

"I need to sit down and have a drink," he said.

James told us later he had been terrified that the scanner would break again, and TSA might take the piece he had out of his bag and begin to question him as to what it was and why it shut down a TSA X-ray machine.

I ordered James a glass of water, and we all sat and recovered. Although it had been stressful, this last episode seemed to seal a camaraderie that had been building for the duration of the trip. We were an unlikely team: two scientists who believed they had physical evidence of off-planet intelligence, and a professor of religious studies. It was unlikely, but being with them felt right. Tyler and James were perfectly willing to share their knowledge with me, even though they knew I was agnostic about their artifacts. To be honest, both James and Tyler felt that the science had to be the answer to potential origins of the artifacts. Until then, it was exciting potential that might lead to an understanding. And potentially an artifact of hierophany. They never felt that I disrespected them, and they respected that I, just like them, was on a quest. Their quest was different from mine, but we were united in our desire to know more—as much as we possibly could know—about the phenomenon.

JAMES

Master of the Multiverse

> Do you believe then that the sciences would have arisen
> and grown if the sorcerers, alchemists, astrologers
> and witches had not been their forerunners?
>
> —FRIEDRICH NIETZSCHE

A CONTENTED CHIHUAHUA LOLLED ON James's lap as we
spoke about our trip to the site scheduled for the morning.
James and I drank beer, and Tyler sipped water. The sun had
set and the sky turned an icy blue color as the full moon
slowly rose, its beams reflecting off the white desert sand.
This eerie, beautiful setting cast a spell on me. The rainbow
that had greeted us upon our arrival seemed like a gate of
colored light through which I had entered into a part of the
country that was somehow more alive than North Carolina,
where I lived. I had the uncanny feeling that the place was
somehow conscious that I was there.

"I consider belief in the phenomena to be an IQ test,"
James explained as he stroked the little dog's tan fur.

"If a person cannot fathom the possibility, as far as I'm
concerned, they haven't passed the test. They're not smart
enough, and I don't want to talk to them about this subject
area. I consider their minds closed," he said.

This was typical of the James I had come to know. To say he didn't suffer fools gladly would be an understatement. He eviscerated them, took them apart limb by limb with the sword of intellect. I had witnessed this on several occasions. The victims were always worthy opponents, such as other top scholars from universities like Princeton. I felt bad for them because James usually humiliated them beyond the point where he had won the argument, but I also understood his motivation. He and certain members of his extended family were lifelong experiencers. He interacted with the phenomenon on a personal and professional basis. He saw the best and he experienced the worst of it. His dismissal of and scorn toward those who didn't believe was personal. He was also protective of many others he knew who were actively and sometimes brutally victimized for their belief. Critically, his own belief was forged in the crucible of evidence. As much as I was intimidated by James's intelligence and passion, I saw him as a hero. He had the guts and the ability to take on anyone in the world who dismissed the reality of the phenomenon. He fought the good fight, for the right reason: because he believes—or as he would say, because he *knows*.

MEETING JAMES

James was the first scientist I met who was also "out" as an experiencer. He was also in a rare category as an academic who studied the phenomenon. My colleague and I had heard that he might be interested in attending a small get-together of like-minded colleagues. We did some background research on him. What we found blew our minds. He held an endowed chair of molecular biology and headed a laboratory at one of the top universities in the world. He was a successful inventor. He had a global reputation for pushing the boundaries of science and biotechnology. In our correspondence with him, we were astonished by his openness. He was very transparent about his interest in the phenomenon, and he seemed, at least in email, devoid of pretention. He was a top dog but acted like a regular guy. I liked him already.

I first met him in person at our summer conference in the foothills of Northern California. The tastes of professors tend toward the conservative and economical, so it was startling to see a high-end roadster, tricked out with a red leather interior, pull up outside the small hotel where we were to meet. A group of us were standing nearby and silence fell over us as we watched the car park. Out popped James, sneakers and all. He apologized for being late. The style of his entrance, probably typical for Silicon Valley millionaires, presaged our introduction to James and his extraordinary work. It proved to be a wild ride.

JAMES: EXPERIENCES AS A YOUTH

At dinner that evening, I made sure to sit next to James. I offered him some wine, and he related his experiences with the phenomenon, which began in his childhood. When he was five or six years old, he recalled, little people would appear in his room. They stood by his bed or looked at him through his bedroom windows. He insisted that he was awake when these events took place, and he said emphatically, "I was not asleep. Oh, and I was paralyzed." He complained to his parents, who told him that he had had some bad dreams. Yet, he told me that he knew that these night visitors were real.

Later, as a young teenager, he had a strange encounter while delivering newspapers on a paper route. One of his customers, Mr. Jameson, demanded that his paper be delivered by 5:30 a.m. every morning. If James didn't make it in time, he might lose his route. One morning, as he frantically pushed himself toward Jameson's house, he realized he wasn't going to make it in time. He sometimes took a shortcut through the woods, though he had always felt apprehensive about the area. But he was already late, so he had to use the shortcut. As he entered the forest, things just didn't feel normal. A shapeless formation of lights slowly passed over him, just above the treetops. It was about twenty feet across and completely soundless. He felt frozen in a time warp of light, bright as the sun, with no apparent source except itself. James just stood and watched in awe. It came and went in less than ten seconds. James kept his paper route, but from this point onward he completely avoided those woods.

Nothing happened again until he was in his thirties. One night he woke up from a sound sleep and saw a tall, thin presence at the end of his bed. It was smoky and translucent. He did not feel afraid, even though he was, again, paralyzed. In his head, he heard the words "Go to sleep." He did.

When he had arrived at our small hotel, the room James was given had a window that wouldn't close all the way, and there were no shades. He made it clear to the proprietor that this was unacceptable. Later I realized that James had developed a fear of open windows in childhood and it was now a compulsion. He needed to close the windows and cover them up with curtains. A close relative, he said, suffers from the same fear. Once, as a teenager, James pranked his relative by drawing a picture of a scary face and posting it on her window. The prank went very wrong. Upon seeing the face, the girl turned white and asked James, "How did you know?" For years afterward he wondered about her reaction.

After the incident with the presence in his bedroom, a chance occurrence opened James to the possibility that his experiences were related to UFO phenomena. An avid reader of science fiction, James picked up a book by Harvard researcher John Mack, *Abduction: Human Encounters with Aliens.* James at first thought the book was fiction. He was shocked by what he read. The experiences of Mack's subjects were exactly like his own. They described night visitors who paralyzed them and seemed to watch them in their sleep. The beings also spoke to the subjects telepathically. Mack had gained notoriety for his claim that the experiencers were psychologically healthy and that the experiences they described were common. He saw this as a significant cultural development that demanded serious scholarly attention.

By the end of the book, James realized he was reading what amounted to the story of his life.

A NEW RESEARCH DIRECTION

James knew that he had to embark on a research direction that had no path, no predecessors, no mentors. Luckily, he was already distinguished for this style of research. His colleagues would scoff at the seemingly impossible ideas and hypotheses he proposed at conferences, but then he would "leave them in the dust" in the lab and make his ideas real. James was already a pioneer. On the agenda now was a new research direction in which he would grapple with his past and with one of the most significant questions in human history. In fact, at this stage in his life, there was no other agenda. Although he kept up with his day-job obligations and grant proposals, the new agenda would dominate his life and seep into every aspect of his thought processes.

James surveyed his colleagues. He didn't know anyone who was an experiencer, nor was he acquainted with Jacques Vallee or anyone else who studied the phenomenon scientifically. All good science is done within communities of peer review and analysis, so James knew he needed to find like-minded researchers. But where? This was a field in which he knew no one. He came up with a daring plan. He decided to put himself on the map, to "out" himself publicly as being interested in the phenomenon. He began by reaching out about a spectacular case: some recently found material that was claimed to be of alien origin. James said that he could determine the truth of this claim. His plan proved to be a good idea, and a bad idea.

Any serious researcher of UFO phenomena is aware that many governments have engaged in programs of "perception management." There are good reasons for this having to do with national security. Sighting events could have to do with another government's military program, or, if the strange crafts are really from off-Earth, they might be hostile. Or—most likely—governments do not want to cause alarm and they just don't know what UFOs are. In the words of the philosopher Ludwig Wittgenstein, "Whereof one cannot speak, thereof one must be silent."

In any case, there is an exhaustively documented history of perception management. Declassified documents reveal that governments, including in the United Kingdom and the United States, have often covered up and managed information about reported UFO events.[1] One of the most famous instances of this can be found in what is known as the Durant Report, an account of the proceedings of the 1953 Robertson Panel, a US government committee convened to study UFOs. Although the committee concluded that UFOs in and of themselves did not represent a security risk, they recommended a project of perception management that they termed "training and debunking": a mass-media education campaign, enacted with the help of academics and media moguls, to control public knowledge about UFOs.[2] The report concludes:

> This education could be accomplished by mass media such as television, motion pictures, and popular articles. Basis of such education would be actual case histories which had been puzzling at first but later explained. The Jam Handy Co. which made World War II training films (motion picture and slide strips) was also suggested, as well as Walt Disney, Inc. animated cartoons. It was believed that business clubs, high schools, colleges, and television stations would all be pleased to cooperate in the showing of documentary type motion pictures if prepared in an interesting manner.[3]

What this means is that the phenomenon is usually portrayed inaccurately, either intentionally by government sources or unintentionally by producers and directors creating products to appeal to consumer tastes. Only serious researchers know this. Everyone else, for the most part, assumes that what they see on television in documentaries or in the newspapers is being reported accurately. James, a top researcher in the hard sciences but not in UFO phenomena, reached out to several public ufologists, one of whom claimed to have access to an artifact that some claimed was supposedly not of this earth—or at the least not understood in accepted science. James knew that if he gained access to this artifact, he would be able to analyze it and determine its origin. He also knew that his involvement would be publicized and attract the attention of people who might be serious researchers. His ultimate goal was to meet them.

James contacted the ufologists and they agreed to let him examine the artifact. It certainly looked anomalous, and it had features that were not readily explainable. The ufologists would include James's research in a documentary watched by millions of people. James would conduct the experiments at his university in his spare time, and the ufologists would film him and report his findings—whatever they might be. Advertisements and media about the documentary hyped his participation and suggested that his findings would change science. James, however, had only said that he would ascertain whether the artifact was from Earth or elsewhere. He did not assume that it was of an alien origin. But he did want to know what caused it to have such anomalous features.

At one point during the experimentation, James became convinced that the specimen was assuredly from Earth. Using the tools of his trade, the data pointed strongly that it was of human origin. His conclusions seemed lost on audiences, however, and even on several ufologists with whom he was working. Media focused on the artifact as having a non-human, alien origin. The public thought James had confirmed that it was alien.

The media pronouncements on James's research were so confusing that he decided to work with a few credible, high-profile science publications and newspapers to make a more direct statement on the matter. These publications affirmed that James had debunked the claim that the artifact had an alien origin and emphasized that he had in fact found it to be of human origin. Yet, even this well-meant attempt to correct the story missed the point. James is a scientist. He used his skills to show that something that appeared anomalous could be understood within the parameters of natural processes. He ruled out that the artifact was from "elsewhere." It could be understood by conventional science. That did not mean he ruled out the reality of the phenomenon of UFOs. That phenomenon, he believed, was very real. This artifact was not an example of it.

THE VISIT

James's reason for affiliating with the more public ufologists was to achieve a goal—to meet serious researchers of the phenomenon so he could carry on with his new research agenda. He needed a community of researchers who played by the rules of science and peer review. Soon after the much-publicized event, he met with success. The serious researchers actually came to him, but his introduction to them was extraordinary and frightening.

The title of the television series *Punk'd* had become a part of everyday, ordinary vocabulary. Being "punk'd" by one's friends meant that one was the butt of a practical joke while simultaneously being filmed and even streamed in real time online or, worse, on television. It was, to some, an honorary humiliation. James, who lived in a university town, was aware of the show and had seen a few of his friends get punk'd. When the men in black suits knocked on James's office door, he opened it and stared into two very grim, unhappy faces. Who are these people? he wondered. The men asked if they could come in and talk to him about the artifact and "other things." James wondered, "What have I gotten myself into this time?"

He invited them into his office, and they accepted the invitation, not saying another word. The silence felt to James like a vague sort of threat. He made a joke to lighten the mood, but the men did not respond. After James offered them some water, he decided that he would match their cold demeanor.

"What is it that you want?" he asked.

"We want to know what you really found out about the artifact."

"I already stated many times I can't find any evidence it has an alien origin."

"We already know that. We want to know why you got involved and what else you might know."

After a moment passed, James came to the conclusion that he was most likely being punk'd. Amused, and ready for the charade to be revealed, he looked around for evidence of a camera or film crew. There was none. Hmm. With neither side knowing exactly what the other knew, there ensued one of the most interesting conversations of James's life. One of the men turned out to be, like him, a top researcher at one of the world's most renowned universities, but with a long association with intelligence agencies. The other man was with a large aerospace firm. What started as a disturbing encounter became a meeting of minds.

The two visitors seemed grim and serious primarily because their own research into the phenomenon had proved to be very disturbing. They dealt with radiation effects and other biological interactions of the phenomenon with humans, a subject of which James knew nothing.

As they talked, he realized that the serious researchers he'd been looking for had arrived, and they weren't who he had thought they would be. Instead, they were very much like him and not public ufologists. They were not the "Men in Black." They weren't interested in publicity. But they were very interested in helping people who needed help. Over the next several months, his two (fully human) visitors exposed him to a nontraditional path that was as much a science as what he practiced at his "day job." James had found his peers.

James related his story and his experience of the "men in black" over wine at the conference dinner. I was riveted. He explained, "I have seen things that our current theories of science cannot explain, yet the evidence for them is very real, as real as anything that the current theories support. I tend not to throw out evidence, even if it doesn't fit. In fact, I think what has made me successful is this very strategy, to not ignore what doesn't fit, what doesn't make sense. That type of evidence, the type that causes researchers to scratch their heads, is the type that is most attractive to me, and what has taught me the most. So, I know we are not alone. There is something here; what does it want? Is it studying us? I don't know. But it is here; there is no doubt in my mind."

THE SCIENTIST

James gave his presentation to our little group the next day. We filed into a small conference hall, which was lit by beams of warm sunshine that streamed through its tall windows. We filled our small white coffee cups and settled into our chairs. James was ready with his computer. We made ourselves comfortable and prepared to hear the young scientist who had arrived so flashily in his high-end chariot.

As James unveiled his first slide, we all squinted to decipher the object pictured. None of us recognized what it was. It turned out to be a photo of a massive molecular microscope, something that none of us had ever seen before and probably would never see again. It was giant—like no microscope I had ever seen. It looked like a big, shiny, hospital CAT scanner. James's lab had built it. From that point onward, we all knew that we were witnessing a level of research that was beyond anything we had seen before. I wondered where this presentation could possibly go from here.

Each one of us had studied the phenomenon and was well acquainted with the relevant case studies, which were of individual sightings or of a flap—a series of sightings of UFOs by several individuals and even groups of individuals over a span of a few days. These case studies provided evidence of an aerial phenomenon that was anomalous. "Anomalous" was the word indicating that we had ruled out its being known aircraft or drones or blimps, that it was not attributable to military exercises, and that it often left physical traces such as burn marks on objects or grass—or people. Several of us had already presented case studies from the historical record that appeared to correlate with modern cases. It was clear that there was a range of beliefs among the attendees. Several presenters were of the opinion that the phenomenon was psychological and that it involved imaginary projections, by people or groups of people, onto unexplained external stimuli. An example of this could be that a group of people spotted a blimp that they mistook for a UFO, and due to their specific group dynamic they projected onto it the interpretation that it was a hostile alien craft. The presentations made in this spirit were convincing. Other presenters were convinced that the phenomenon was a form of nonhuman intelligence that wasn't necessarily extraterrestrial but may be interdimensional or coexisting within our own universe, though in a different frequency. These presentations were just as compelling. The questions we had been pondering were all over the map: Was the phenomenon something that arose within the social imaginary? Or was it secret advanced military craft? Was it truly something nonhuman? We were all academics, and even though we were researching something that was considered to be on the "fringe," we were well trained to follow the conventions of our respective disciplines. The standard baseline from which we all functioned was pretty conservative: unless we had proof that it was nonhuman, we would refrain from advocating that hypothesis.

Like a gust of fresh air, James's opening statements completely and unequivocally transcended our stoic provincialism. As we examined his pictures of the microscope and sipped our coffee, he blindsided us with this assertion: "We will start by stating that the phenomenon commonly referred to as UFOs exists. The evidence supports that there is a phenomenon, it interacts with humans, but we cannot as yet explain it. However, we can identify its effects *on* humans and the physical channels of communications through which it operates. Through studying its modes of interaction with us, we can gain considerable knowledge about it."

This claim caused the hairs on our well-trained academic necks to rise. We were now wide awake—and not because of the coffee.

To scientifically capture all these experiences or events, argued James, the people predisposed to having them—that is, to being contacted by nonhuman intelligence—must be studied. The literature shows that contact manifests as anomalous experiences, as telepathic communication with aerial objects and beings, or as anomalous cognition (knowledge of future events or other knowledge for which there is no conventional explanation). It also manifests as random sightings of aerial phenomena that sometimes interact with witnesses through such things as "beams of light." The Bible and records from Catholic history and other religious histories are replete with accounts of such events. James's own experiences and those he had recently learned about from his relatives informed his theory, but he had also studied others who reported them. As a scientist, he was aware of two things, one explainable, the other not. His research found that some people exhibited knowledge of events for which they should not, according to what we know about normal processes of acquiring information. He could not explain this, but he relied on quantum theory to suggest that particles distant from each other seem to have knowledge of each other and even affect each other ("spooky action at a distance"). And scientists don't know why this is so. He suggested that perhaps there is a quantum field of information and somehow his subjects tap into it. He theorized that the ability to contact or be contacted is likely to be genetically determined. Since genes define structures and architectures of the tissues of the body, genes would underlie the components of a brain receiver for such information. He said, "Once the phenomenon contacts humans, from wherever it originates, it leaves a signature. That signature is traceable. It is physical, physiological; it is processed then in a world that tools of science can study. We can identify it."

James speculated that once the information is received by the brain and recognition occurs, it likely creates changes in human physiology—somewhere a neuro-electrical channel is modified, and the signal enters a world that scientists can access. That means researchers can identify the most obvious changes and trace them back to their molecular roots. He explained that because form and function are linked in biology, the function of the brain has strong genetic components—driven by the architecture of the neurons as defined in the genetic instruction set in a given individual. Genetics, by definition, is familial, and experiencers of the phenomenon often run in families—like his.

James's presentation was fascinating and intensely personal. He revealed that he knew some people who were "bedeviled" by the contact events. Contact was not always welcome. I listened carefully to the words James chose. Bedeviled was used more than any other word in this context, but other words were "harassed" and "bothered." "Bedevil" means to torment or harass maliciously or diabolically. It became clear to me, if not to the other attendees, that James's mission was personal, and it was heroic. He was out to develop a medicine, an antidote, to the malicious contact event. James was incensed that contact took place on "their" terms and not on ours. James's plan was to shift that relationship by 180 degrees. He wanted to give humans the right, and the ability, to say "no." As the day progressed, I began to wonder whether this was now James's primary life mission. It was no wonder he would not tolerate equivocation with respect to the reality of the phenomenon. To say it wasn't real was to discount James on several levels—intellectually, certainly. But more personally, it discounted the suffering certain experiencers endured—some their whole lives.

When James ended his presentation, a silence filled the room. I imagined that the others had as many questions as

I did but were still formulating them. Or maybe they were too shocked to speak. In any case, a colleague finally ventured a question that I shared, which had to do with quantum theory and James's idea of the field of information. "At what point does the anomalous phenomena come into contact with human hardware?" James repeated the question in his answer. "Basically, it appears that anomalous cognition starts on a level that is beyond the physical world of which we are aware. I suggest it is on some quantum level. Humans use their senses to interact with energy forms like light. Modern physics reveals that at these well understood physical levels quantum information is transferred. However, once an individual becomes aware of an anomalous event or knowledge, it has at that point already been transferred into human brains as a "recognition" via mainstream physiology—namely, human neuronal hardware. So, let's identify where this information is transferred, and identify what types of molecules are involved in this process. This allows us to begin the long road towards identifying the human interface that is our connection to the phenomenon.

"I can use cutting-edge approaches to locate these molecules and to identify the signatures of interaction," he continued. "This is the same kind of science that drives biomedical research in the world today. Just as certain intellectual traits are heritable because of how the brain is wired, it should be assumed that so is the ability to interface with the phenomenon. Therefore, it would be a good idea to locate families where the trait is dominant. It is assuredly a 6th sense that is associated with a material component we already possess."

As James was speaking, I thought about my own family. A cousin in law enforcement has always possessed what

I believe would conform to James's definition of anomalous cognition. His abilities have helped him out of many dire situations where his life or the lives of others were in danger. One of my students, José, a Marine and author who has seen active duty, wrote about it in his book about his experiences on the front line. "I always found it fascinating when seniors in the Marines would say, 'Your point man, if he has a knack for finding IEDs or sensing things, keep him there,' and we always did, even amongst one another. In training they called it atmospherics, but observing the physical components of your surroundings was always secondary, even tertiary."[4] It was pragmatism, not just simple belief, that determined whether or not "the sense" existed. When your life or the life of your friend is on the line, you're not about to argue metaphysics. If "the sense" works, then use it.

The "sense" existed for James because he had evidence of it. He had been exposed to communities of people who displayed anomalous cognition—some of whom suffered terribly for it. Although he did not go into the particulars of the cases he researched, at one point he did look at me and say, "Diana, you know how you've studied the history of Catholicism? And they called some entities either angels or demons? Some of the interactions seem benign—and even helpful. Well, the behaviors of some of the things I am talking about would have been called demonic, as short as one hundred years ago." I thought of his use of the word "bedeviled" and shuddered.

James reminded me of Tyler. Perhaps Tyler was preternaturally gifted with anomalous cognition. Perhaps the founders of the American and Russian space programs were all gifted, or cursed, with various forms of anomalous cognition. I thought of all the strange anecdotes I had read

and heard about the founders of these programs, like Jack
Parsons or Konstantin Tsiolkovsky, both of whom believed
that nonhuman intelligences were sending humans sym-
bolic messages, but that only some humans were able to perceive these and translate them into products. Tsiolkovsky
suggested that it was the creative geniuses, scientists, and
poets who were able to receive the communications. Qian
Xuesen, a Chinese engineer who helped establish Parsons's
Jet Propulsion Laboratory and China's ballistic missile program, also believed in an energetic force that imparted information, Qi (Chi). Of course, Qi has a long history in Chinese
and other Asian religious and philosophical traditions as a
sacred life force that can be tapped with the right training.
Though not aware of Tsien's history of trying to utilize or
successfully utilizing Qi to promote science, Tyler certainly
adopted his own set of physical "training" practices to tap
into what he thought was a nonhuman intelligence.

I have read several excellent histories of science, but
I have yet to read the history of *unorthodox* science. Annie
Jacobsen's book *Phenomena* is an excellent overview of
some of the most recent unorthodox ways in which science
is conducted in the United States. She focuses on the US
military's experiments into remote viewing, parapsychology,
and similar phenomena. During the conference break,
I thought through the strange tales I learned as a graduate
student. There was the case of Srinivasa Ramanujan, a poor
boy from the Indian province of Tamil Nadu. He had only
some elementary training and education in mathematics,
yet went on to be one of the most brilliant and innovative
mathematicians of the early twentieth century. His brilliance
was so astonishing that there is a journal devoted to his novel
ideas, which are still being worked out and understood. How

did a young boy with little training in mathematics end up at Oxford University and become recognized as one of the most brilliant mathematicians in the world? He attributed his brilliance to the Hindu goddess Lakshmi. According to Ramanujan, she whispered mathematical equations in his ear and provided him with specific calculations. This explanation embarrassed his colleagues at Oxford. But he never backed down from his story. To him, it was the truth.

I asked James where he thought he himself derived his extraordinary creativity. He seemed pleased that I asked him this question.

"The young are usually the ones who ask me this question so directly. I am invited all over the world to give lectures about my lab's research. Graduate students are the only ones who have ever asked me how I get my ideas. And truly, it is pretty simple, and somebody needs to study it—document how people do it. I have told them that I think creativity can be trained and that there is a process.

"Usually I lay out the most recent problem I need to solve in my head, sometimes just before bed," he continued. "I think of all the possible parts of the problem that I can. What is the question, what would the perfect answer enable, what is a practical answer? What pieces of things could possibly go into 'making' the answer? Then, I just ask the subconscious processes in my head, which I laughingly refer to as little 'elves,' to work on the problem while I sleep. You can call them elves, but I don't know what they are—I used to think they were just some version of the subconscious processes that help you navigate a room of people while talking to a friend or trying to avoid an overly chatty colleague at a party. Call them anything you want. Either I wake up with the answer or out of the blue it just pops into my head in the next few days, more often just after waking. And I know I am not alone in this. But the point is, there is a process and I think it can be trained. I am beginning to wonder if the information comes from somewhere else at times—because for the life of me I can't figure out from where the inspirations arrive sometimes. I seem to be given a part of the puzzle for a problem to which I simply did not previously have access. I wonder sometimes if the ability is somehow related to brain structure and the phenomena."

"Wow." I was envious. That sounds so easy, I thought. It also sounded like a protocol, somewhat like the one Tyler had told me about.

There was a very interesting process of creativity going on in Tyler's and James's cases, and in the cases of people like Ramanujan and Qian. I had read recent research about creativity that showed that the parts of the brain that correlate with identity get shut down when a person is performing a creative act. This causes the individual to associate the act with an external agent. Was this happening in the case of Ramanujan or the others? But if so, what of the physical traces and artifacts that both James and Tyler studied? These seemed to solidify the processes, for each of these men, onto a real external agent, not just an imaginary one.

"James, can you explain a little more about these elves, or that place where you think this information is derived?" I asked. "Is this the same place where the quantum information exists?"

"Not sure," he replied. "I do know that friends of mine who are scientists often report that they learn things when they sleep, almost as if they travel to some place and come back with information that helps them in their research.

I have no evidence for any specifics, except that the ideas do come, and I am not entirely sure of how the answers arrive so neatly packaged."

THE PROCESSES
OF TRANSLATION

Tyler seems to be able to tap into an ocean of creative ideas and bring them to tangible fruition as biotechnologies, but he was never able to explain how the process worked. James, on the other hand, is the consummate professor—a teacher. He could explain how he accomplishes seemingly impossible feats, and he could document and describe the process. His presentation laid out a formula for how anomalous cognition could derive from some potentially nonmaterial, ethereal information field and then be translated into human hardware.

Jacques Vallee had theorized such a direction for research. James, like me, counted Vallee as one of his major influences and mentors. In fact, Jacques was among the serious researchers who reached out to James when he publicly outed himself as interested in the phenomenon. (Jacques was not one of the men in black. That is not Jacques's style.) Jacques and James formed an instant bond. In James, Jacques found someone capable of understanding his theories and even hammering out their scientific details. In Jacques, James found an entrée into the community of the best researchers of the phenomenon. James once observed that "Jacques has achieved his status precisely because he has never concluded the phenomenon is anything specific. In fact, Jacques has infuriated most ufologists because he won't fall in line. All

Jacques has ever claimed is that the phenomenon seems infinitely variable. Every time you claim it is one thing, he shows you twenty counter-examples. But, per Jacques, the overarching message the phenomenon appears to send is 'you are not alone'—styled to the level of your cultural understanding and abilities."

Jacques, one of the first truly innovative thinkers on the subject, suggests that the UFO might not be an object, but some kind of "window" into another dimension. The window metaphor is quite interesting, as a window *is* a physical object but one through which we see into another place. Could the *hardware* of James's subjects be like this, physical yet somehow like a conduit, or windowlike?[5]

I decided to introduce Tyler and James. They had so much in common. They both felt they knew the phenomenon was real, both worked in the biotechnology sector, and both were at the top of their fields. James studied the biological hardware of human capabilities for anomalous cognition, whereas Tyler studied the material hardware— the supposed crashed alien spacecraft. I predicted that once they met, they would become fast friends and decide to work together.

When I returned home from the conference, I received emails from each of them. One was Tyler's invitation to the site in New Mexico. James had sent me a few pictures of a fancy charity gala in the Los Angeles hills, showing him dancing with the beautiful pop star Katy Perry. He was obviously having a wonderful time. Nothing could trump that event, except my invitation to him to attend the site with me in New Mexico. James would have traded a thousand dances with Katy Perry for that simple opportunity.

THE SITE: JAMES AND
THE AFTERMATH

I first introduced the two men over email; I wanted James to come to the site with me and Tyler. After Tyler decided that James should go to the site, realizing that I wouldn't go there without him, they started an email correspondence that led to a working relationship, just as I had anticipated. Tyler invited James to his home laboratories. At first, they kindly kept me in the correspondence and phone calls, but soon they were working so closely that I was left behind. By the time we traveled to New Mexico, they were already close associates.

Tyler and I arrived in New Mexico before James, so we picked him up at the airport. James's schedule is packed with international travel for talks at universities and other invited visits, yet I could tell when we picked him up that this was the highlight travel moment of his year. The excitement was evident on his face, and he couldn't suppress his smiles. I was happy too, but not for the same reason. I was still suspicious of the whole thing. My role was to document how the site impacted the belief systems of these scientists. I wasn't suspicious of James. As a fellow academic, even in a completely different discipline, I knew that we shared a common set of assumptions and values. We valued transparency, as long as it did not endanger anyone, as well as honesty and peer review. The last is basically a process whereby other smart people can call out our work for errors or stupidity, obliging us to correct or defend it. These were the ethics we followed. Tyler's profession was so opaque to me at this point that I wasn't sure how to relate to him. I valued James's presence on the trip because I knew that he would be able to help me assess Tyler.

That evening, Tyler related a brief history of the site. It was the site of one of the crashes that occurred in New Mexico in 1947, but had been largely forgotten over time. It was not the Roswell event. There were some eyewitnesses. Tyler knew one of them, who had been a child at the time. Tyler told us that the site had a particular "feel" to it, and that whenever he had traveled there, inevitably people would get into fights, whether due to the intensity of the situation or the "energy" of the site itself. Maybe Tyler was preparing us for this; I wasn't sure. I certainly was not going to fight with him or James. The last time I had "fought" with anyone it was with my brother and I was twelve.

"I've never been to the site without feeling the energy," Tyler whispered.

James and I listened. This wasn't typical field research.

"The last time it was between the eyewitness and a scientist who we took out there," he said. "Nobody really knew what it was they were even fighting about. They probably didn't even know. They almost came to blows. The place will work on you over time. You will see."

I could tell that James was more interested in this than I was, and I soon found out why. Later that night, giving us an overview of his own research, James indicated that sometimes the phenomenon acts like a contagious agent. Once it attached to a given individual, it would sometimes spread to others who came into contact with that individual. This information, coming from James and not just Tyler, was disconcerting. I prayed that night for protection—from what, I wasn't sure. But I prayed.

The next day, when we arrived at the site and our blindfolds were removed, James and I were both struck by the stark beauty of the place, made more vivid by the brisk wind that whipped through the desert valley. The site was spread across several acres. James and I took several opportunities to confer while Tyler was busy with something else. We had both been convinced on some level that we were being set up. Later that afternoon, when James found the artifact, my commitment to the theory of a setup weakened, although it would never completely disappear. James's metal detector had indicated something down between the rocks. He spent some time digging and even after all that effort had to reach far down into the rubble and weeds to retrieve the material. The material looked like crumpled tin foil that was also a type of fabric. It was clumped with dirt and debris.

James's preliminary analyses of the materials, months later, made it hard to believe they were made on Earth. In fact, he said he wasn't sure, given their structure, that they could be made anywhere—and certainly not on Earth in 1947. That's how weird they were, and how they defied conventional explanation. They were just . . . anomalous.

The ensuing analyses of the material had a significant effect on James's and Tyler's beliefs. Although Tyler was already convinced that an extraterrestrial craft had crash-landed at the site in 1947, James's analyses further justified Tyler's belief. Really, James didn't know what they were, but he knew that they were genuinely anomalous. It didn't matter to James whether a craft had crash-landed at the site or whether Tyler (or someone else) had planted the materials for me and James to find. The artifacts *potentially* substantiated that something material associated with the phenomenon could be studied or confirmed. James could not understand how on a multiacre site he had been able to find this structured object. For James, his side interest and hobby now took on a very different flavor.

Having studied religion for many years, I can offer the following observations. First, here are two eminently credible people—scientists no less—claiming that there are artifacts whose provenance is truly unexplainable. This amounts to having the testimony of credible witnesses, which is pretty much what one finds in the first written documents of Christianity and Buddhism. The Christian Gospels are the testaments, or testimonies, of credible witnesses—the apostles, which is a Greek word that literally translates as "those who are sent," or "messengers." Second, the credible witnesses are attesting to something truly unexplainable, truly anomalous. In religious studies, this would be a miracle, either a miraculous object or a miraculous event, such as a healing.

Of course, this is not how James or Tyler would speak about the site, but it is my assessment. The sites in New Mexico function as sacred sites for a new religion, the religion of the UFO event and, as I will argue, the religion of technology. They are the places of a hierophany, where nonhuman beings descended to Earth and left us a "donation," as James, chuckling, once called it. It was something for us to ponder, a window to another reality too obscure to fathom now, but evidence of the "other." James and people like him will eventually crack its code. I was reminded of the first scene in the film *2001: A Space Odyssey*. A group of hominid human ancestors are losing a fight with a rival tribe. After a night's sleep, they wake to find an anomalous object, the monolith. The monolith, and the idea it inspires, drives them to develop one of the first tools of war and is the catalyst for human evolution and dominance. Arthur C. Clarke's insight is compelling: not all ideas are benign gifts.

What do I think about the artifacts? And the site? I believe that James's analyses are correct. They are artifacts and accomplished scientists cannot understand them. Do I believe that they were delivered, either intentionally or unintentionally, by extraterrestrials or beings from other dimensions, that is, nonhuman intelligences? This is where the story gets complicated, and *religious*.

Suffice it to say that although James and Tyler don't know who or what produced them, their instruments and analyses seem to confirm that the artifacts should not exist. The pure impossibility of their findings motivates the pursuit of their unorthodox science, which, James reminds us, is as real as what he does in his day job. Tyler and James are very comfortable in the gray area of not concluding, of not knowing what it is they found; it is what prevents them from making dogmatic, and even ridiculous, assertions, such as that these are spacecraft debris from Mars. They both leave open the possibility that the materials are of human origin, perhaps from some military program. Like Socrates before them, they show that they are wise by admitting that they do not know. That doesn't prevent them from trying to find out— because the truth probably is out there.

THE MYTH BEGINS

When I got back to North Carolina, I realized that I had inadvertently walked into some version of the "myth" of what has become known as the Roswell event. I was never interested in the topic of UFOs until 2012, and so knew nothing about the conspiracies and theories surrounding Roswell, New Mexico, beyond what the general public knew. I knew it was a place where UFO enthusiasts believed an alien spacecraft had crashed in 1947, but that was it. Because of my training, I knew that the town functioned as a pilgrimage site for believers and people who wanted to believe. Coincidentally, I am writing this during the annual Roswell UFO Festival, which is a four-day festival expected to attract over fifty thousand people this year. Its social media pages are filled with pictures from the alien-costumed pet event. It is a carnival.

I was aware that my experience with James and Tyler could lend support to the myth that alien technology had been found in New Mexico. My question became, How could I write about the two scientists and what they found and believed without inadvertently folding myself and my own story into the already-existing, convoluted, mind-bending myth of Roswell? The practical answer was that I could not prevent this.

James said that if the parts came from a crashed non-human vehicle of sorts, then it was a gift or donation for us to figure out. Tyler's interpretation of Roswell was different. Tyler was always fond of saying that the best place to conceal the truth was in a mess of confusion. In other words, a lot of covert things could have happened or could still be happening around Roswell and Area 51, and the UFO narrative was a good cover story for it, or a way to camouflage it. Because of the myth, reasonable people would scoff at any news associated with that location. It was a good way to keep such people from looking into it. Of the books that I had read about the topic, two struck me as relevant, but for very different reasons. Additionally, they were completely different sorts of books. Annie Jacobsen's *Area 51: An Uncensored History of America's Top Secret Military Base* strikes me as probably correct on one count, namely, that there are top-secret military programs going on in and around that area. Tyler's hypothesis that the UFO carnival masks this activity makes sense to me. The other book is *The Day After Roswell: A Former Pentagon Official Reveals the U.S. Government's Shocking UFO Cover-Up*, by Philip Corso. It suggests a completely different story. Jacobsen is a journalist and does not in any way affirm the reality of UFOs or of nonhuman intelligence. Corso, on the other hand, insists that there really was a crash in New Mexico and that it was his job to disseminate the debris and parts from the alien vehicle to private industry, with the story that they were advanced Chinese or Russian technology and that it was our duty to reverse-engineer them to produce whatever technologies we could. Whereas I tended to believe Jacobsen's narrative, I felt as if I was living within Corso's. I decided that, on some level, both accounts were true. It was Tyler who brought me to this conclusion.

"Roswell is difficult because not only do humans not understand what is going on within the topic of nonhuman intelligence, but the topic has been intentionally confused and aggravated by some other forces, human and possibly nonhuman. Also, two people can have a first-hand credible experience and both of them not agree on what they witnessed. Humans don't like to admit to themselves that they can't figure things out, so we tend to be pretty arrogant about our abilities. But I've noticed over the years that progress is fairly incremental, and many have died not figuring anything out. For me, I've tried to use it mainly as creative inspiration and a force within me that is bigger than myself which has good intentions and seems to serve the greater good—almost like reading science fiction, except like in the movie business where a show that is based on a true story seems to carry more energy and attraction to people. I get enough of the truth to keep my vision and inspiration going. I've helped a lot of people heal, so I know it is a good force."

This brought me back to two ideas of how the artifacts functioned. I thought of Jacques Vallee's idea of the UFO not being an object, but a window through which we might view other worlds. The myth of the crashed alien craft functioned like this, perhaps. But there was another idea, not necessarily incompatible with the window idea: if the legend and the artifacts that inspired it covered up the truth of the development of secret weapons by the US military, then the legend was also a weapon—a weapon of information, like Kubrick's monolith.

FROM TYLER AND JAMES TO INFORMATION OPERATIONS

The interesting commonality between James and Tyler is that each had anomalous experiences and each believed he had come across anomalous materials but refused to draw conclusions about them—except that the materials were anomalous and couldn't be explained by the tools they possessed. This is not generally how experiencers proceed. People like answers. Answers come through interpretation.

One thing that UFO events and religious experiences have in common is that they don't begin as UFO events or religious experiences. They *become* UFO events and religious experiences through interpretation. I have not met one experiencer who has seen an anomalous aerial object and immediately thought, That is a UFO! Usually they think of all the things it could otherwise be: a falling star, a satellite, a weird airplane, secret military aircraft, a special holographic video produced by tech-savvy neighborhood teenagers. Nobody wants to be known as the person who has seen a UFO, so, if they see something anomalous, they usually choose the least unlikely explanation and leave it at that. The same is true of religious experiences. People who have reported experiences that are ultimately deemed religious have at first been confused by what they see or hear. It is not immediately clear to them that they are having a *religious* experience. A good example of this is found in the *Book of Samuel* in the Hebrew Bible/Old Testament. The young Samuel is asleep one night when he hears his name being called. He wakes up and assumes that it is his teacher, Eli. He awakens Eli, who says he didn't call the boy. It happens again, and again Eli says that he didn't call. When it happens a third time, Eli interprets it as a calling from God and tells Samuel to listen to it and to respond. Samuel's experience then becomes an important religious experience that confers upon him the status of a prophet.

There is an important, although not absolute, distinction between the event and the subsequent interpretation of it, and how the event becomes embedded within a tradition of meaning. Ann Taves has proposed a building-block approach to understanding how events become religious events. A variety of disciplines that include cognitive science, sociology, and history can help explain the processes by which people identify their experiences as religious, or as being related to UFOs. These reveal that human perception is informed by a wide range of things, including what we think we know or should see. From childhood, we are trained on how to see, as well as on what not to see. One example in the book *The Invisible Gorilla and Other Ways Our Intuitions Deceive Us* illustrates this point quite humorously. The authors, Christopher Chabris of Harvard University and Daniel Simons from the University of Illinois at Urbana-Champaign, showed a group of subjects two videos of people passing a basketball. They were asked to count the number of passes. In one of the videos a person wearing a gorilla suit makes an entrance and walks slowly through the basketball players as they pass the ball to one another. Chabris and Simons found that half of the subjects did not notice that an enormous gorilla had passed through the scene. How could this be? How could someone miss seeing a huge gorilla walk slowly through a basketball game, or anywhere for that matter?

The cognitive science of media suggests findings that are even more disturbing than missing a gorilla in one's midst (although if the gorilla were real, maybe not). What one sees on a screen, if it conforms to certain criteria, is interpreted as real, even if it is not real and even if one knows it is not real. Screen images embed themselves in one's brain and memories; they can determine how one views one's past and even determine one's future behaviors. This research has disturbing implications with respect to belief. What we see, we tend to believe. The conventional means by which truth is established—that is, by evidence, credible sources, and historically accurate corroborating testimony—is wiped off the plate with one rich, visually stimulating and emotional image. The creation of a belief system is now much easier to accomplish than it was two thousand years ago, when people didn't possess smartphones and were not exposed to the ubiquitous screens of a culture that now teach us how to see, what to see, and how to interpret what we see.

Jacques Vallee once told me emphatically, "Trust no one. Do not even trust what you see." Some years earlier, the well-known scholar Donna Haraway had asked me to think about what was happening in my brain and my mind when I looked at images on film, or in the minds of people who witnessed apparitions of the Virgin Mary. "What is happening in your mind, or their minds, during these events?" I hadn't a clue then. But when Jacques told me not to trust what I was seeing, I knew what he meant. From my own research, I knew that digital media and media of all forms are manipulated to produce a specific response that is desired by the producers for purely economic reasons. I was beginning to research the ways in which virtual and digital media were being used for political purposes under the auspices of information operations: how the military employed media, social media, and all types of electronic media for purposes of national security. All of these media have played major roles in the creation of global belief in UFOs and extraterrestrials. It is in the world of media that the myth is created, is sustained, and proliferates.

IN THE FIELD

The War Is Virtual, the Blood Is Real

> Believe no one. Believe nothing.
>
> —JACQUES VALLEE, personal communication

> Space might be the final frontier, but it's made in a Hollywood basement.
>
> —RED HOT CHILI PEPPERS

"TALK TO ME FACE-TO-FACE, AND I will show you what I think of debunkers!"

The threat, posted on social media, devolved from that point into a series of very specific descriptions of bodily and emotional harm. It was directed, by name, to Scott Browne. Scott reacted with bemusement, as he had seen it all before. The crime? Scott had demonstrated that a photograph that a poster had claimed was a real UFO was actually a Photoshopped object.

"Debunker" is not the worst name one can be called in the field of ufology, but it is pretty close. It describes a person who doesn't believe in the phenomenon and actively discredits people who claim to have witnessed something anomalous in the air or in space, including some trained observers, like pilots. Scott Browne has been called a debunker—and far worse than that. In fact, the names he has been called are not fit to be printed. Yet they have been posted on Facebook, on Twitter, on YouTube, and in internet forums. Scott Browne is a hated man, for all the wrong reasons.

Scott is a debunker and a true believer. He is a debunker *because* he is a true believer. He is a talented graphic designer and professional videographer, which means that he has the skills to determine whether the objects in photographs and videos are truly anomalous, computer-generated imagery (CGI), or lens flares. These skills happen to be the skills of the new soldier, because today, wars are waged on several fronts and virtual reality—a misleading term—bleeds into the world of skin and bones. Physical and virtual worlds intersect and permeate one another. Scott Browne has seen the rise of the virtual UFO—and its profitable hoaxes—and he has intuited the disturbing consequences of its development: for all intents and purposes, the fabricated UFO is the real UFO. Yet Scott resists and fights its existence because he believes there is a real thing. He is a true believer. He and the trained observers in his international group, *In the Field*, believe they have photographed the real thing. Significantly, he has had anomalous experiences suggestive of UFO activity from the time he was a toddler.

As a historian of religion, I know a vocation when I see one. A vocation, from the Latin *vocatio*, means "to be called" to perform a special task, usually a sacred mission. It has traditionally been associated with religious orders, like the priesthood or the call to become a nun or a monk; it is also associated with the sense of being called to perform a task or to become an artisan or craftsperson. Scott has been gifted, or cursed, with a vocation, and like many vocations, it is uncompensated—at least monetarily. The rewards of a vocation are typically spiritual, which may be hard to remember when one is on the front line of ufology, attempting to bring common sense into an arena that is a true carnival of hoaxes, consumerism, and misinformation. The weariness of the fight, the threats, and the slights to his name and reputation have made Scott want to quit. In the short two years that I have known him, he has wanted to walk away from this work innumerable times. But he keeps coming back. He cannot stop his work, his sacred task. It won't let him go.

Scott is the creator and moderator of *In the Field,* an international study group of trained videographers, photographers, and graphic designers who also study the UFO phenomenon on a regular basis. The group is located on Facebook. Its members use their skills to try to identify anomalous aerial objects. By identifying CGI and the common lens flares that are often mistaken for UFOs, they also provide a public service. They rule these things out in the effort to preserve an accurate record of truly anomalous objects. They identify hoaxes and "out" hoaxer websites. If any of the members are found to have hoaxed a photograph or video, they are removed from the group. The members are bound by a code of ethics and a methodology. If they deviate just one bit from these codes, Scott deletes them. Several times I've witnessed hoaxers removed from the group and they always react with a whirlwind of vitriol and bitterness.

I learned of Scott's group from friends who told me that their videos were genuine—that is, they were recordings of authentically anomalous phenomena. I wanted to join these skilled researchers to see what they had filmed. I wasn't a videographer or a photographer, so I wasn't sure that Scott would let me in, but one day I approached him on Facebook and asked if I could join. He asked about my credentials.

I told him that I studied UFO phenomena, and then, on the chance that he might respect Jacques Vallee's work, I told him that I was a fan of Jacques and that I worked with him. That was credential enough; he immediately let me into the group, for which I am grateful. The work being done by its members and the issues that get raised demonstrate the processes involved in the formation of a dogma. The members aren't dogmatists; in fact, they are just the opposite. Each of them is trying to stop (or at least slow down) a huge, indiscriminate tidal wave: the momentum of media coverage of UFO phenomena. The movement of the wave begins with a witness with a high-tech video camera who documents an anomalous phenomenon. Then, it gains momentum on the internet and social media. It becomes virtual, something dogmatic and orthodox—something, it seems, in which everyone believes, and something far removed from what it was, originally. This is how media technologies inform UFO belief.

"What is your position on religion?"

I am sitting across from Scott at a trendy coffee shop in Northampton, Massachusetts. Northampton reminds me of my original home in Northern California. The rich smell of good coffee permeates the air, and I am enjoying the break from the sweltering humidity of the North Carolina summer. Scott asks the question carefully. I can tell that he doesn't want to offend me, but he needs to know my answer. He wants to know if my mind is closed, if I am dogmatic. The question is a fair one, and one that I get often. Because I am a professor of religious studies, many people naturally assume that I am religious. People in my field study religion, of course, but they are all over the map with respect to their personal beliefs and practices. Most of the atheists I know are also professors of religious studies. That is not me, however.

"I believe there is a truth, Scott, but I am open about what it is. I go to a Catholic Church, but I started out as a born-again Christian when I was eleven years old, to the surprise of my parents. I believe in practicing those things associated with the traditional religions, like honesty, charity, things like that," I answered.

This answer seemed to satisfy him. I realized that he asked about my religion because he wanted to trust me but knew he couldn't if I was clinging to a dogma that wouldn't allow me to open my eyes and see what appeared right in front of me. The study of the phenomenon requires an open-minded, nondogmatic approach.

Scott almost apologized. "I seem to have this ethic, this . . . UFO ethic," he said.

He didn't know how much I understood, and appreciated, that ethic.

"I formed the group because I had been studying the phenomenon, photographing it, taking videos, etc., of discs and other aerial objects, and I knew there were a lot of other people doing exactly what I was doing, who were from all over the world. We would post our videos in forums and groups on Facebook and in other places. The problem arose because our videos of authentic stuff would get posted side by side with videos that were obviously hoaxed. The owners of those videos would say things like, 'This is a UFO from the Galactic Federation of Alpha Centauri' or something like that. I was so discouraged, because I was trying to proceed to study the phenomenon in a way that was systematic, and, well, none of us were getting anywhere. My question to those posters was, 'How do you know where this is from? Did they tell you? What evidence do you have?'

"I talked about this with researchers that I trusted, like David Stinnett. They each also worked like I did: they went out into the field and captured objects on photos or on video that they then scrutinized. These were the people I wanted to talk to. I established *In the Field* basically so I can meet these people, and I stipulated certain criteria for membership.

"The group was formed for people who are actually pursuing and witnessing the phenomena on a regular basis with video cameras and a variety of high-tech equipment. It is also for serious researchers who are interested in the study of what these observers are doing and capturing. There are three requirements to join:

1. You must shoot your own footage/stills of anomalous objects on a regular basis and be able to present them to the group (YouTube or other).
2. You must be familiar with the basics of the study of this phenomenon.
3. You must keep an open mind with no preconceived notions about the nature of the phenomenon (angels, aliens, demons, galactic federation, etc.).

I made sure to state that the group is not intended for those who wish to fuel the perpetual machinery of hoaxes and disinformation that make our work much more difficult. We do three things: we observe and study; we document and capture; we share. I don't accept anything that is CGI, false info, disinfo. We don't want anything that reeks of a bad sci-fi movie. We encourage common sense."[1]

SCOTT'S EARLY EXPERIENCES

When I asked Scott why he was interested in the phenomenon, he spoke of his childhood. He was careful to say that the things that happened to him then may or may not be connected to his obsession with UFO phenomena, although he has an inkling that they could be. When he was barely three years old, he somehow disappeared from the family home. His father, a police officer, was frantic when he and his wife couldn't find their son. He immediately issued a missing persons report, and a massive search was mounted for the toddler, involving the police department and the whole town. Scott was found, many hours later, in a nearby field. When his mother frantically scooped him up, he said that he had been talking with the cows that lived in the pasture. His mother, writing in her diary, said, "Scott gave everyone a scare at 5:30 this morning when he decided to take a walk on his own. I was so worried! We are still not sure how he managed to get out of the house but some friends ended up finding him down the street coming from the field and he was so excited that he talked to the cows even though they were horses!"[2]

Scott's brother, who was two years younger, recalled experiencing recurring dreams about his older brother throughout his childhood. In these dreams, he would see Scott on a table, hooked up to machines, surrounded by people with big heads who were examining him. Scott also had recurring dreams, in one of which he saw a giant praying mantis looking into his window at night. He actually kept a praying mantis as a pet for a time.

These events faded in Scott's memory as he grew older, until 1987, when they were revived by a series of disturbing experiences. Just after getting married and moving into a new apartment complex, Scott experienced a series of episodes of sleep paralysis. One night he sensed the presence of a being close by his bed. It was menacing, and as he tried to wake up, he found that he was completely paralyzed. The same thing happened to him again a few nights later. This time he told his wife.

"I think our house is haunted."

She tried to reassure him that he had just had some bad dreams. Scott wasn't buying it, however, as the feeling was too real to him. The disturbance to his normally mellow attitude lingered for days. During a visit to a bookstore, as he browsed the aisles, a book seemed to pop out at him. The title of the book was *Out There: The Government's Secret Quest for Extraterrestrials*, by Howard Blum. There was one blurb on the book's cover, written by Whitley Strieber. It said: "Absolutely essential reading."

"I read that book and others," Scott said. "And it felt like, for the first time, I understood my past. The book is written by a serious journalist who reports that the topic is being studied by the government. It put all of the past events in context. I'm not saying that those things really happened, but I'm not saying they didn't either. Reading the book gave me the impetus to begin my work, that is, to record the objects I saw in the sky, and that is when I started this research.

"In the beginning, I made a lot of mistakes. I just believed what I saw in the photos other people took. I didn't think they would hoax the pictures. But I was gullible and naive. I was already a graphic designer, so it was really easy for me to spot a faked photograph. Unfortunately, I began to see that almost all the photos were Photoshopped or hoaxed.

"Also, a lot of people I began to meet told me that I needed to be hypnotized to uncover what happened to me as a child. I did a little research on being hypnotized and regressed, and I realized that you can create false memories. I said 'no thanks' to that. I decided that it was better to not know than to know something that wasn't true or never happened."

Scott's desire to identify anomalous photographs and evidence motivated him to keep his online group free from hoaxers, and even free from parts of the ufology community that were not exactly hoaxers but could nevertheless do harm by harassing people who want to know the truth.

"VISITORS FROM SOMEWHERE ELSE"

As *In the Field* became better known, it started to attract refugees from the internet—people who were actively pursuing UFOs by capturing videos of orbs, discs, and other aerial phenomena that couldn't be identified as planes, drones, blimps, or other natural objects and events. One such refugee was a woman from Pennsylvania named Alison Kruse. I call her a refugee, and that is not an exaggeration. She sought refuge from harassment: she had been called a liar and a hoaxer, and her computer was targeted with viruses. *In the Field* was, for Alison and others, a refuge from the dark side of the virtual world of ufology, where the harassment and denigration of its own members are rife.

Alison's introduction to the phenomenon occurred in 2008, when her daughter told her that she had seen a strange, glowing red plane hovering around their house in the early hours of the morning. Alison asked her to draw a picture of the "plane" and saw that it was saucer shaped. Her daughter had never been a fan of *Star Wars* or *Star Trek* or any of the other television, movie, or internet media about space or extraterrestrials, and Alison was excited by her sighting, considering it possibly a once-in-a-lifetime event. It wasn't. A few months later, as the sky was getting dark, Alison looked up and saw what she thought were the planets Venus and Mars. Planets, unlike stars, do not twinkle. She continued to watch them and realized that they were twinkling brightly, and she wondered, Why would these planets be twinkling brightly like this, like stars? Then they moved and one just faded out. This struck her as something impossible. Perhaps, like her daughter, she had seen a once-in-a-lifetime phenomenon?

"Then, one after another, it kept happening," she said. "Soon after that I heard the kids banging on the windows and screaming bloody murder. While they were outside sledding in the snow they had seen a cigar-shaped object hovering in the sky. Then we kept seeing more objects, during the daytime and at night. Finally I realized that these once-in-a-lifetime events kept happening. Soon after that I met the researcher Bruce Cornett, and he said that the sightings would increase. Well, they did."

Witnesses and researchers often report the strange feeling that once you become aware that there is a phenomenon, it becomes aware of you. They report that the first sighting is just that—a first—and then others follow. The uncanny feeling that the objects are aware, or watching those who are watching them, is common. The starlike objects began to appear more frequently to Alison and others near her. She decided to upgrade her camera and video equipment so she could document the phenomenon more accurately. She spent thousands of dollars on better equipment, including night-vision cameras. She also started to share her videos with the public on YouTube and other social media, as she thought that others would be interested in her findings. She wasn't prepared for the vitriol and harassment, and she didn't understand it at all.

"I thought that people would be interested in seeing these strange objects. Other people, in other parts of the world, were posting about similar types of objects too, but they didn't get harassed. I am not sure why I did."

Alison proceeded in a systematic fashion. The objects would fly around her house and over the forests near her home. She would video-record them and then call the Federal Aviation Administration (FAA) to find out if there were aircraft flying during the times she had recorded. Researchers of UFOs can and often do obtain these records.[3] When she learned that there were not, she was excited. She invested even more money in better equipment and waited to see the objects. In November 2010, she filmed a starlike object over the forest and then called the FAA, as usual. They confirmed that there were no aircraft in the sky when she recorded her object. She got a copy of the data disc that the FAA had put together of the event. It was titled "Murrysville UFO."

Because Alison was recording so many of the objects, she was able to determine their patterns and behaviors. Early on, she said, she noticed that they would mimic conventional airplane lights.

"I thought to myself, They are copying our lighting arrangements so they can imitate us and not be recognized."

She also noticed that they seemed to be aware of her too. On her YouTube channel, she posted an open invitation to others to come and watch the objects and video them. She said that when people took her up on her offer, they noticed that the objects seemed to disappear when Alison grabbed her video camera.

"It was funny. They seemed to be shy or something."

Alison thought it was strange that people from all over the world were posting videos of aerial objects that behaved in ways that were similar to the ones she was observing.

"To me, this counters the theory that these objects are secret military planes or craft or black operations. That theory might be true if they were being seen just here in the US, but they are coming in from everywhere—Australia, Europe, Pakistan, everywhere."

After many years of observing her "punks," as she calls the objects, she speculates about what they are and why they are here. Like Scott, and Tyler, and James, she admits that she ultimately doesn't know.

"It seems as though the starlike objects are actually their vehicles, the things that they travel within. These sometimes open up, kind of like a zipper, and let other, smaller objects come out of them. Neither me nor anyone who has observed them with me has seen a being emerge, nor has a being or anything from them ever communicated with me. Maybe there are no beings associated with them, and they are purely remote-controlled. Maybe they are like our Mars rovers: they are sent here to gather information for beings who live somewhere else. I don't know. Maybe they are from our future and are our future selves, and that is why they can't communicate with us, because they would change our present and their own history if they actually did make contact. Maybe that is why they don't communicate with us."

For Alison, one thing is clear. Her life took a dramatic turn when she discovered that her house and the forest near her house lay under a very busy sky. She felt a duty to document the objects that flew in and around her neighborhood. The once-in-a-lifetime opportunity that had one day presented itself became an almost daily occurrence, and it also became her passion.

"I had to document and record this. This is history. We are being visited by visitors from somewhere else."

UFOS ARE PHOTOGENIC

Scott reached into his bag, pulled out a folder, and placed it on the table between us.

"These are my best captures," he said.

There were two photographs of an aerial object, partly hidden within clouds. He had blown up the capture by several degrees, each displayed in a separate box for me to view. I studied the images. I saw a metallic-looking, somewhat round object that looked like a classic UFO (Figure 3.1).

I recalled Carl Jung's remark that flying saucers are not "photogenic." Jung was responding to an encounter much like mine with Scott; he was confronted with the testimony of a worthy and honest man and it made him wonder about the topic. He went on to write his book about flying saucers. For him, they were not just a rumor or just a myth, but a *living myth*. He also called it a *universal mass rumor*, which, he said, was "reserved for our enlightened, rationalist age." Jung wrote:

©2013 Scott Browne - 11-9-13 Western Ma.

FIGURE 3.1. Scott Browne's picture of unidentified aerial phenomenon.

Considering the notorious camera-mindedness of Americans, it is surprising how few "authentic" photos of UFOs seem to exist, especially as many of them are said to have been observed for several hours at relatively close quarters. I myself happen to know someone who saw a UFO with hundreds of other people in Guatemala. He had his camera with him, but in the excitement he completely forgot to take a photo, although it was daytime and the UFO remained visible for an hour. I have no reason to doubt the honesty of his report. He has merely strengthened my impression that UFOs are somehow not photogenic.[4]

Almost seventy years have passed since Jung wrote this. He was correct about the American propensity to document and record events with their cameras (today, their cell phones). Since the 1950s, UFOs have become photogenic, a fact to which the work of Scott and the members of his group attest. Jung did, however, offer a valuable methodological approach that addresses photographic evidence of UFOs, its dissemination, and its link to the formation of mass belief. He was writing in the 1950s and the internet had not yet been invented, but this new form of information dissemination became the key that would unlock and help us understand Jung's prescient speculations.

Jung was apparently ill at ease, if also excited, about the prospect of studying the UFO. "Every man who prides himself on his sound common sense will feel distinctly affronted" by reports of UFOs, he wrote. This, however, would be a mistake. "Psychologists who are conscious of their responsibilities should not be dissuaded from critically examining a mass phenomenon like UFOs." He proceeded to carve out a method for studying the phenomenon. That method was predicated on first denying that there was a real UFO. "The apparent impossibility of the UFO report suggests to common sense that the most likely explanation lies in a psychic disturbance."[5] The site for the proper study of the UFO was thus within the human psyche.

At this point Jung introduced his concept of "amplificatory interpretation." By this he meant a process that an individual or a group engages in when confronted by an unknown object, in this case an aerial object. This also applies to objects in dreams or visions. According to Jung, the meaning of the object "has to be completed," because at first it is confusing—like the confusion Alison felt on that night in 2008 when she thought she was looking at the planet Venus. After it blinked and faded out, she said to herself, "What the hell was that?" She was confused.

Jung wrote that the UFO was *apparently* impossible. He didn't say it *was* impossible. His point was not necessarily to dismiss its objective reality, but to move the study of it into the realm of the psyche, his field of expertise. It was a methodological strategy. Jung missed an opportunity to note that it is the potential physical reality of the UFO that causes it to be a *living myth* and a *universal mass rumor*. It is both a myth and a potential future reality. He nods in this direction, noting that contemporary physics has revealed so many scientific truths that appear miraculous that "UFOs can easily be regarded and believed in as a physicists' miracle."[6] Its realism is what gives it its bite. It is also what makes it religious. Religions work because practitioners believe in their truth or truths, even without overt evidence to support them. Religious truth, practitioners point out, exists independent of belief or disbelief. This is just what billionaire Robert Bigelow said when asked if he was afraid that people might think he was crazy because he admitted that he believed in extraterrestrials: "I don't care. It's not gonna make a difference. It's not gonna change the reality of what I know."

Jung's choice of the word "apparently" is echoed by contemporary media about UFOs. The soundbites for *The X-Files* convey a similar attitude toward the potential reality of the UFO. The meme "I want to believe" does not express belief, but the desire to believe. Belief is postponed. "The truth is out there" performs the very same function. The truth is somewhere, but not here, not now. It will be here someday. That the truth is postponed does not make it false; it makes it future-real. Thus, the first takeaway from Jung's speculations (of which he was guilty!) was the proposition, if only as a figure of speech, that the phenomenon was potentially real.

The other takeaway has to do with the notion of amplificatory interpretation, or the creation of the meaning of the UFO after the initial confusion of seeing one (as well as before seeing one). The people I have interviewed have resisted it in every way they could, but it is impossible to resist entirely. Seventy years after Jung's analysis—well before Scott, Alison, James, Tyler, or I was born—everyone has been subjected to the universal mass rumor of the UFO. It is something from which none of us could possibly escape. We have all been exposed, from childhood and throughout our lives, to media about the UFO, both as entertainment and as a possible reality, as when it surfaces as a topic on local news stations. How does one come to deem an anomalous event a "UFO event"? Often this is facilitated by a book encounter.

THE BOOK ENCOUNTER

Each of the people I interviewed who said they believed their anomalous experiences were connected to the UFO phenomenon had had a "book encounter." At some point after their experiences, which sometimes persisted over half a lifetime, they were given, came upon, or in some perceived miraculous way were directed to read a book that put their experiences into perspective and seemed to explain them. Arthur Koestler describes the serendipitous arrival of the very book one needs when one needs it as the experience of "the Library angel."[7] It was Carl Sagan's book about the cosmos that changed Tyler's life and started him on a path of fusing what he learned in the space program with his ideas about biotechnologies to form companies that helped heal people. The book appeared mysteriously in his luggage, at a point in his life when he was lost and desperate. For James, the book was John Mack's *Abduction: Human Encounters with Aliens,* which he picked up on a whim, believing it to be science fiction. The book read like his own biography. It helped him frame his experiences as being related to UFOs. Scott's book, *Out There: The Government's Secret Quest for Extraterrestrials,* popped out at him while he was walking through a bookstore. Although this is not surprising—he was in a bookstore, after all—the book was unlike anything that he would have chosen to read, yet he felt compelled to read it. Echoing James's experience, the book seemed to Scott to read like his biography, and triggered the processes whereby he started to piece together his obsession. The book encounter differs from the library angel experience in that the books offer the readers an explanatory framework for their experiences.

One doesn't have to accept the book's framework. Scott's care and sophistication with regard to his belief structures, qualities he says he did not possess in the beginning of his research but forged over time, are instructive. It shows how anomalous experiences become connected to a cultural narrative. As I studied his photographs and placed them back on the table, Scott offered his observations.

"After I read the book *Out There,* and numerous other books, I thought differently about the experiences I had as a child. Really, I could not avoid the fact that they were so similar to what was being reported by people who said they were abducted and whose stories were in the books like *Out There.* But I also knew that I didn't know this beyond a doubt. I could not, honestly, make a direct link between my childhood experiences and the aerial objects I started to record.

"But, intuitively, I think there is a link."

Most people are not as careful or as restrained as Scott. If they have had anomalous experiences and they happen upon a book that seems to explain them, they will assume that their experiences relate to the theory presented in the book. This is a normal process, and it is what Jung was getting at when he proposed the concept of amplificatory interpretation, in which the unconscious amplifies the associations related to an image or a group of images and creates a meaningful framework that is then associated with events or experiences. It is partly how cultural narratives are produced, and while the concept appears reductive, it is not. It admits to a real, objective event; it just refrains from identifying, with certainty, what the event is. Instead, it focuses on the meaning projected upon and associated with the event.

I have delved into the processes of the creation of the UFO cultural narrative elsewhere.[8] I've interviewed Edward Carlos, a professor of art whose anomalous experiences were featured in John Mack's book *Abduction*. He resisted the term "abduction" so strongly that I felt the need to rewrite and publish his experiences from his perspective. His story and its subsequent publication illustrate well the process of first experiencing anomalous events, then determining "what" they are, and ultimately determining what they are called. Carlos (as he likes to be addressed) noted that while Mack was attentive to his feelings, he felt that Mack never had a grasp of the real phenomenon. Carlos used the language of several traditions to illustrate his experiences. He said the light beings he encountered were sometimes like angels and sometimes like aliens, but that they transcended the language of both Catholic and contemporary UFO traditions. Yet his experiences became UFO related for a wide audience after the publication and success of Mack's book. Carlos never called his experiences abductions or said they had to do with UFOs, but that is how they were understood after Mack's book framed them that way.

In my article, I described the experience of St. Teresa of Avila, a sixteenth-century Catholic nun. An extraordinary woman, she instigated such significant change for the Catholic Church of her time, both theologically and socially, that the modern church bestowed upon her one of its highest honors: Pope Paul VI made her an official "doctor" of the church, a title previously held almost exclusively by men. In the beginning of my shift away from researching Catholic history and toward modern-day UFO events, I revisited Teresa's own testimony about one of her famous anomalous events. Her status as a mystic began with a most unusual occurrence, which even she had a hard time understanding. It is commonly referred to as the ecstasy of Teresa, or the "transverberation" of St. Teresa, which means "to be pierced through." She wrote about it in her diary:

> Beside me, on the left hand, appeared an angel in bodily form, such as I am not in the habit of seeing except very rarely. Though I often have visions of angels, I do not see them. They come to me only after the manner of the first type of vision that I described. But it was our Lord's will that I should see this angel in the following way. He was not tall but short, and very beautiful; and his face was so aflame that he appeared to be one of the highest rank of angels, who seem to be all on fire. In his hands I saw a great golden spear, and at the iron tip there appeared to be a point of fire. This he plunged into my heart several times so that it penetrated to my entrails. When he

pulled it out, I felt that he took them with it, and left me utterly consumed by the great love of God. The pain was so severe that it made me utter several moans. The sweetness caused by this intense pain is so extreme that one cannot possibly wish it to cease, nor is one's soul then content with anything but God. This is not a physical, but a spiritual pain, though the body has some share in it.[9]

I had read this account many times. An angel pierces Teresa, and she goes into a religious ecstasy. That is how I had always read this passage. After I had my realization that modern UFO reports were in some ways similar to historical accounts of religious phenomena, I decided to re-read some of the primary sources from Catholic history. My new reading proved very interesting. I had never paid attention to the fact that her description differs radically from most of the artistic representations of it. There are paintings and also a famous sculpture by Bernini. They depict Teresa near a little angel with a small dart. They do not depict the illuminated nature of the small being, nor do they show Teresa's confusion about the being (why it was real, and not imagined, which would be difficult anyway). I was particularly struck by her confusion. She doesn't know how to interpret this being. Is it an angel? And why is it different from the angels she has seen in the past? To think through this event and make sense of it, she turns to the books of her time, Catholic angelology, which was known by her confessors, the men in whom she confided. Her book encounter, facilitated by her confessors, helped her understand her experience as religious, having to do with Catholicism and God.

The book encounter is one step in the process of determining that anomalous experiences are related to UFOs or, as in Teresa's case, to God and religion. In these examples the medium is a book, but it could very well be a movie or a documentary that provides the explanatory framework. Interestingly, these two interpretations—that the experiences are related to religion or that they are related to UFOs—are by no means mutually exclusive. There is a "biblical–UFO" hermeneutic that provides a way to interpret these experiences as being both religious and related to UFOs. Several religious groups, such as the Nation of Islam, are informed by such a strategy.

Eddy, an experiencer I met, saw no problem conflating UFOs with biblical events. I met Eddy at a local UFO conference where he related his experiences. He said that he regularly saw flying saucers, usually in formation, and always fifteen or more, though often nobody around him could see them, leaving him as the only witness. For a year he tried to get his wife to see the saucers, and finally she did. She even caught them on camera, producing ten pictures of the saucers. He had brought a magnifying glass to the conference so we could get a good look at them.

When I asked him what he thought of these visitations, he asked me if I had read the Bible. I certainly had, I told him.

"Then you should already know what these are," he said, surprised.

"I might know, but please explain."

"Jesus went up in the clouds on a saucer, and he will come down again just as he went up," he explained.

Some theologians read the Bible in a similar manner. For them, the UFO or flying saucer is equivalent to aerial phenomena mentioned in scripture. In the late 1960s, Presbyterian minister Barry Downing advocated for this interpretation in *The Bible and Flying Saucers*. The Reverend

Michael J. S. Carter, a graduate of Union Theological Seminary, offers a contemporary version of this claim. His book, *Alien Scriptures: Extraterrestrials in the Holy Bible,* argues that the Bible is a history of human contact with extraterrestrials.[10]

SYNCHRONICITY AND THE UFO EVENT

They've always been a reality; what they are is still a theory

—DAVID STINNETT

One of Scott's mentors and inspirations is David Stinnett. David has been a UFO researcher for more than thirty years and served as the director of the annual New Jersey UFO conference. He has been a student of the Bible for over twenty years, and he is a Christian. He is an active field researcher who travels to hotspots of activity with his video equipment, the deployment of which is guided by the years of knowledge and experience he brings to his work. David, of all the researchers and scientists I met, is the least likely to draw any conclusions whatsoever about the phenomenon. His influence on Scott helped *In the Field* maintain its rigorous standards.

"Many years ago I was going about my business on an ordinary day in New Jersey. I was on a back road in central New Jersey. I then saw a gun-metal-gray aircraft. It looked exactly like a C140 transport. It was creeping up very slowly, and that caught my attention. It was completely silent. I exited my car with my camera. When I tried to capture the object in my finder, it would not show up. I jumped back into my car and tested the camera on other objects. My camera was just fine. I jumped out again to capture the image, and the thing was gone.

"I went home and walked into the room where I keep a library of UFO papers, white papers, research, books, and lots of information. Instead of grabbing what was most convenient, like something on the top of the pile of papers, I reached under a huge stack of papers and wrested out a VHS tape. It was a video of Dr. Bruce Cornet giving a lecture to the New Jersey UFO Congress. In the video, Cornet described, in perfect detail, the craft I had just seen."

There was a pause in our interview. I said, "A synchronicity."

"Yeah, a synchronicity." He said this deadpan.

I could tell that he wasn't buying it. He had related an event that was like a book encounter but involving a VHS tape, but he wasn't taking the bait. I found this refreshing—and fascinating.

"Synchronicities are one aspect of the phenomenon," he elaborated. "If a researcher does not experience them, he or she is not really doing the research right. But—and this is important—a researcher doesn't have to accept that the synchronicities mean anything. They need to be careful, because synchronicities are very convincing when you experience them. They could lead you off the right track, and the right track is to not be convinced.

"We see orbs, or we see unexplainable craft, and most people jump to the conclusion that it represents extraterrestrials from outer space. I don't make that jump.

"One aspect of the phenomenon, pointed out by Vallee as well as by George Hansen, is that it tricks and deceives.[11] Researchers, when they encounter the real phenomenon, are so amazed by these aspects of it that they go off the deep end in their theories and conclusions. They are convinced that only they have these meaningful synchronicities. These very real experiences dupe them into believing that the phenomenon is what they think it is. Well, it's not."

Synchronicity, as defined by Carl Jung, is the coming together of inner and outer events that are not causally linked but are very meaningful to those who have the experience. The UFO community is not the only community that experiences synchronicity. In my research into Christian communities, I found that many people interpret synchronicities, or meaningful coincidences, as signs from God, or meaningful events that show them that they are on the "right path in life." David's position on experiences of synchronicity was atypical; he did not assume that they meant anything deep or profound. He certainly was aware of them, however.

I had been introduced to a similar position of restraint in the midst of having a full-blown synchronicity. After college I had tried to read the philosophy of Friedrich Nietzsche. His work had come highly recommended, but the passages I read always seemed misogynist. After a few pages of reading I would close the book in disgust. Friends insisted, however, that I should try to get past that unfortunate aspect of his work. One friend had given me a copy of *The Gay Science*, which I placed on my nightstand and promptly forgot.

It was New Year's Eve. That night, I went to bed early and fell asleep immediately. At midnight I was awakened by fireworks and the merry-making of New Year's revelers. Amid the noise, I had no hope of returning to sleep, so I picked up the book on my nightstand. I opened it up randomly. The book was organized as a series of aphorisms. I happened to open it to the only three aphorisms in the whole book devoted to New Year's Eve. The first was titled "Sanctus Januarius" (Saint Januarius or Holy January). I knew that Nietzsche was referring to the miracle of St. Januarius, whose dried blood is preserved in a capsule and every year on New Year's Day is taken out and miraculously liquifies. Nietzsche used this miracle as a metaphor for his own experience of having his life transformed, apparently on New Year's Eve, from dead and dry to profoundly alive. The next aphorism was about how on New Year's Eve Nietzsche declared that he would affirm life, no matter what it would bring him—*amore fati*, the love of fate. So here I was, on New Year's Eve, and I had randomly opened the book to aphorisms about New Year's Eve. This struck me as a meaningful event. Indeed, it was a synchronicity! As my friends had predicted, I was sucked into Nietzsche's philosophy. I eagerly turned the page to find out what more he would say. What would I find next?

The next aphorism stopped me cold. It was about synchronicities, an instance of which I was currently experiencing. The feeling was uncanny. The book had suddenly become *a scary book*. This aphorism, I knew, would now speak to me personally. And it did. I took a breath and proceeded to read the entire thing:

> *Personal providence* – There is a certain high point in life: once we have reached that, we are, for all our freedom, once more in the greatest danger of spiritual unfreedom, and no matter how much we have faced up to the beautiful chaos of existence and denied it all providential reason and goodness, we still have to pass our hardest test. For it is only now that the idea of a personal providence confronts us with the most penetrating force, and the best advocate for it, the evidence of our eyes speaks for it, now when it is obvious that all and everything that happens to us always turns out for the best. The life of every day and

of every hour seems to be anxious for nothing else but always to prove this proposition anew; let it be what it will, bad or good weather, the loss of a friend, a sickness, a calumny, the non-receipt of a letter, the spraining of one's foot, a glance into a shop-window, a counterargument, the opening of a book, a dream, a deception—it shows itself immediately, or very soon afterwards, as something "not permitted to be absent,"—it is full of profound significance and utility precisely for us! Is there a more dangerous temptation to rid ourselves of the belief in the Gods of Epicurus, those careless, unknown Gods, and believe in some anxious and mean Divinity, who knows personally every little hair on our heads, and feels no disgust in rendering the most wretched services? Well—I mean in spite of all this! we want to leave the Gods alone (and the serviceable genii likewise), and wish to content ourselves with the assumption that our own practical and theoretical skillfulness in explaining and suitably arranging events has now reached its highest point. We do not want either to think too highly of this dexterity of our wisdom, when the wonderful harmony which results from playing on our instrument sometimes surprises us too much: a harmony which sounds too well for us to dare to ascribe it to ourselves. In fact, now and then there is one who plays with us—beloved Chance: he leads our hand occasionally, and even the all-wisest Providence could not devise any finer music than that of which our foolish hand is then capable.[12]

The irony of the aphorism stung. While having a synchronistic event, Nietzsche explained that one should not ascribe to it any deep or profound meaning. If I did, I would be ignoring my freedom and would be in danger of embracing dogmas or, worse, believing in an anxious Divinity that knows how many hairs I possess on my head (obviously a reference to the God of the New Testament). The cognitive dissonance of the event was so great that I have never forgotten it, and here was David Stinnett reminding me that there are people who are steeped in meaningful coincidences and synchronicities yet refrain from drinking the Kool-Aid and believing that they might indicate deep, profound meaning.

David does not draw any overarching conclusions about the UFO phenomenon—other than that it is real and that it deceives—but he believes it is real. After years of studying it, he knows it when he sees it. After seeing some of Alison's videos posted online, he took a trip to her house and witnessed it for himself.

"Oh yeah, Alison's phenomenon is the real deal. When I was out there, so was Homeland Security. She's got all kinds of people visiting her and seeing the orbs and other things out in the skies above the woods near her house."

After my interview with David, he sent me a quote from Carl Jung about synchronicity. I took it to clarify his position, that synchronicity is not such a big deal, and in fact, if you're doing things correctly, it is how the world functions: "Synchronicity is an ever present reality for those with eyes to see."

A NEW TYPE OF REAL

When my research shifted from Catholic history to UFO phenomena, I presented my initial conclusions about its objective "reality" to Jacques Vallee, Jeff Kripal, and a few other academics who were engaged in the research. It proved to be an utterly foolish move. As I know now, one cannot just "conclude" about a phenomenon like this. That's akin to concluding things about something as complicated as gravity or light. Scientists still don't know what makes up gravity or light. The astronomer and director of the Vatican Observatory, Brother Guy Consolmagno, reminds us, "Truth is a moving target," and scientists try their best to identify it. But knowledge is acquired in time and is therefore incomplete. In my foolish attempt to think through the ontological status of UFOs, I had argued that they were real only in a virtual sense. That was my conclusion, and I quoted the French scholar Jean Baudrillard as if that would somehow support my point. Jacques's gentle chastisement was swift: "It is unwise to ignore the ontological aspects of the UFO." My point about its virtual reality was a good one, but, he was subtly saying, ignoring its status as a real, albeit incomprehensible, object was foolish. And as I came to see, Tyler's and James's research suggested that its strange reality produced revolutionary, and very real, products.

Eventually I knew that my task was to document the formation of a new religious form—not to reach ultimate conclusions about the ontological status of its mystery. I worked with communities of people who, like Tyler and James, believed they interfaced with the phenomenon directly. What they were doing was genuinely incredible and led me to seriously consider the realism of their research. I assumed that their work would spawn rumors, as Jung calls them—shoots of information or just hints of information that others would then interpret and spin into stories and narratives that would then constitute the UFO narrative, story, and, ultimately, religion. And indeed, this did and does happen.

But Tyler and James are invisible. Their work, and the fruits of their work, will not appear on Facebook. Scott and Alison are public. They are known. My work with them further helped me see how those who are most involved with the phenomenon, and who are known, work furiously to try to correct the great variety of its virtual lives. This task is noble, but ultimately futile. Just as Teresa of Avila's representations in art and sculpture tell a story but don't tell *the story,* Scott tries doggedly to correct the story, even as he knows it is a losing battle.

Toward the end of my interview with Scott, he got silent. I could tell he wanted to say something, and whatever it was pained him.

"The problem," he said, "is that it is now almost impossible to do my job. The technology that is out there makes it impossible to tell the difference between what is real and what is fake. My videographers and I find it harder to make the distinction if the tools the fakers use are sophisticated enough."

We stared at each other in silence.

I was reminded of a recent incident on social media in which Scott had exposed a series of images of supposed UFOs. The original photographs had garnered a large following. The images were of a distant object that was circular and did not look like an airplane or anything conventionally seen in the sky. Scott took the images, blew them up, and posted them side by side, showing what they really were, which were different types of oddly shaped balloons. He posted these on the forums. Scott knew the phenomenon, and this was not it. These were simply balloons (Figure 3.2).

Scott's intervention prompted an interesting reaction from those who had posted the images. They promoted the photographs as real UFOs, and they also accepted the truth of Scott's exposé. Instead of reaching the conclusion that they had misidentified balloons as UFOs, they said that the UFOs had *disguised* themselves as balloons. For them, the

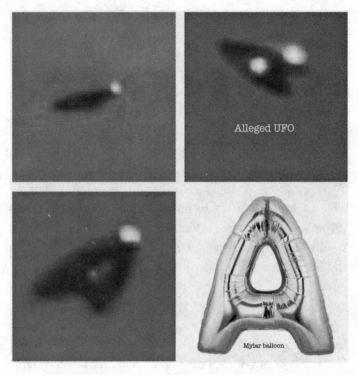

FIGURE 3.2. Scott Browne's balloon/UFO exposé.

objects really were UFOs, but UFOs ingeniously disguised as simple balloons. (They must have read Jacques Vallee's book, *Messengers of Deception*.) This response, though perhaps surprising, is not unprecedented. In the 1950s three Stanford University sociologists infiltrated a small UFO group whose leader, Marian Keech, predicted the arrival of UFOs amid a global cataclysm. Faced with the fact that Keech's predictions did not come true, members of the group concluded that they had avoided the global cataclysm by placing their faith in Keech and her contacts with extraterrestrials. The sociologists had assumed that they would come to disbelieve

Keech, but that didn't exactly happen. Instead, some of her followers reinterpreted the meaning of the events in a way that supported their faith in Keech, and their original beliefs.[13]

Scott told me about another example of how faked UFO photos inform the cultural narrative about UFOs. Early in his research Scott came across a website challenging anyone to fake a believable UFO in a photo and explain in detail how it was done. He used a simple method to show how an "experiencer" was able to create realistic-looking UFOs using ordinary household items (Figure 3.3). In the years following this educational attempt, Scott endured the reappearance of his faked UFO photos in many guises, always represented as a real UFO. Some posters went so far as to identify the places where it was allegedly photographed—all fake, of course. Like the balloon-UFOs, Scott's own faked images garnered a large following. The irony of this was not lost on Scott. He saw how the world of virtual reality eats up the conventionally

FIGURE 3.3. Scott Browne's fabricated UFO.

real and spits it out as something entirely alien—alien, that is, to his original intent and purpose.

Scott and I said our goodbyes, and I returned reluctantly to the sweltering heat and humidity of North Carolina. Based on my work with Tyler, James, Scott, Alison, and David, as well as others, I knew that there was an unexplained phenomenon. I also knew that the cultural narratives about it had nothing—or at least very little—to do with the phenomenon they captured and experienced. The cultural narratives were formed through processes anticipated by Jung with his concept of amplificatory interpretation. Seventy years on, interpretations of the phenomenon were being amplified exponentially through a new social medium that included bots and computer algorithms, not just people. I found myself returning to my original, discarded claim, the one that had humiliated me within the group of researchers: the "reality" of the phenomenon is virtual. But this time, I wasn't implying that this meant it wasn't "real." I had given up the dualism of real and virtual.

THE MONOLITH RETURNS

During our trip to New Mexico, James told me that he thought the artifact we had found in the desert was a "donation," most likely from nonhuman intelligence.

"You mean like the monolith in *2001: A Space Odyssey*?" I asked him at the time.

"Yes."

"Is it good, James? Is the donation for our benefit?"

James was silent as he considered the question.

"It's too early to tell."

As I thought through the objective nature of the UFO phenomenon, I kept returning to Kubrick's film and the monolith. The monolith appears in key scenes throughout the movie, leaving viewers and critics wondering about its message. According to James, a fan of science fiction and of the original book by Arthur C. Clarke on which the movie was based, the monolith is a donation, supposedly from a more advanced species, but its meaning remains mysterious. A clue is given in the beginning scene with the proto-hominids who use it to establish dominance over another tribe. The monolith is perhaps a tool of control. It accompanies humans throughout their evolution, and even on their journeys, through the creation of the artificial intelligence (the computer Hal, in the movie) that eventually leads them off Earth and into the frontier of space. As I watched scenes with the monolith, I realized that it resembled a larger version of my iPhone.

The interpretation of the monolith as a screen, and particularly a movie screen, was first advanced by Rob Ager on his website CollativeLearning.com.[14] Ager studies and creates films and has published an extensive analysis of the symbols of the films of Stanley Kubrick, as well as those of many other filmmakers. In a series of videos, Ager provides in-depth analysis of the visual aspects of the monolith, taking the viewer through each of the varied scenes in which it appears. Ager notes that at one point the monolith even collapses into the movie screen. The monolith, according to Ager, *is* the cinema screen. I find Ager's interpretation convincing. He argues that this interpretation of the monolith excludes reading it as a donation from an alien race. For Ager, the monolith has nothing to do with alien technology. I am convinced by Ager's analysis that the monolith is the cinema screen, but I believe that the monolith can be both the cinema screen *and* the alien. And it is both on many different levels. These two interpretations are not mutually exclusive.

Scott's group exists to erect and sustain a boundary between what they believe to be the real representation of the UFO phenomenon and its clearly faked representations (Figure 3.4). Scott's fear is that advanced media and computer technologies are erasing this boundary altogether. Scott's intuitions are correct, but the problem is intrinsic to the UFO. If one situates the phenomenon within the context of media studies and media ecology, it appears that the digital infrastructure determines and provides an environment ripe for this now-pervasive belief system.

FIGURE 3.4. Scott Browne displays phone UFO apps.

Within a digital landscape, the distinction between the real and the unreal ceases to be meaningful. The loss of this modernist framework gives way to a transcendent one with qualities that appear to collapse or, more accurately, exceed the modern constructions of real and not real. As Jean Baudrillard and others have long argued: real and unreal are no longer meaningful categories or frames of reference. That doesn't mean this framework doesn't exist; it simply means that it is irrelevant to many people. To the extent that theories of UFOs, including extraterrestrials, ultra-terrestrials, and interdimensionality, presuppose a modernist framework of the real and the not real, they miss how these reports emerge from a specific historical context.

The historical shift from modernity to postmodernity and the pervasive effects of the media infrastructure determine and frame our perceptions. I am not throwing out or discounting the reality of the UFO. I suggest that it should cause us to rethink our own constructions of what we consider to be real, because things we commonly take to be unreal in a materialist sense, like movies and video games, have real physiological and cognitive effects. Media technologies have as much an impact on human bodies as biotechnologies, and perhaps even more.

WHEN *STAR WARS* BECAME REAL

The Mechanisms of Belief

MGM is making the first ten million dollar religious
movie, only they don't know it yet.

—ARTHUR C. CLARKE, late 1960s, about MGM's support of
2001: A Space Odyssey[1]

Well, it's not a religious event. I hate to tell people that.
It's a movie, just a movie.

—GEORGE LUCAS[2]

The brain often fails to differentiate between virtual
experiences and real ones.

—JIM BLASCOVICH AND JEREMY BAILENSON[3]

OVER A CUP OF COFFEE, a colleague and I were chatting
about my experience working with the screenwriters of the
blockbuster movie *The Conjuring* (2012). When I originally
received the call, I had only been told that my expertise
was needed for a movie about Catholic culture. It has to be
a movie about an exorcism, I thought. The very first paper
I published dealt with movies about religion, including *The
Exorcist*. At the time, *The Exorcist* was the second-highest-
grossing film about the supernatural in history. Little did
I know that *The Conjuring* would soon displace it from this
position.

"But it is just a movie. It's not real," my colleague said.

"This type of movie produces real physiological effects," I replied, "including practices and belief in things—even supernatural things. They can also create and mimic real memories. In a very real sense, we incorporate these films into our minds and bodies. They become us."

My colleague frowned. "That is very weird. Are you sure?"

"Yes. I am sure."

In that early publication, I had only scratched the surface of how films about religion influence and inform belief. I would later learn that they don't just get in our heads; they *become* us, in the form of memories. I call this the Total Recall Effect.[4] It goes beyond confabulation, the inability to distinguish fact from fantasy—although it could be considered a form of confabulation generated and nurtured by modern technology. My research into urban legends revealed that when people watched movies about religious events, they often assumed they were seeing real events, and they believed the movie versions even if they were not historically accurate. The movie image trumped the historical record.

This was in 2005. I hadn't yet delved into the cognitive basis for these developments, as research into the cognitive science of media and virtual reality was in its infancy. I knew that screenwriters used a particular technique, made popular by the graduate student writers of the screenplay for the movie *The Blair Witch Project* (1999). They increased their sales by pretending that the movie was based on a real event. I was intrigued by this strategy. I knew that something similar was at work in movies loosely based on religious events—movies about Jesus, for example. At the time, I wasn't exactly sure how these connections worked and played out. When I was invited to work with screenwriters who used these techniques, I jumped at the opportunity. It was a stroke of luck to be offered a chance to see up close how they worked. It was also a wonderful chance to conduct some field research.

David Stinnett would be proud that I didn't ascribe too much significance to the synchronicities I discovered when I arrived on the movie set. The screenwriters were Chad Hayes and Carey Hayes, twin brothers from Malibu whose very successful careers were about to get supercharged by the success of this movie. The article I had written was about people just like them. For their part, they were amazed to meet a woman scholar of religion—just like the protagonist of their last film *The Reaping* (2007), starring Hilary Swank. (Who makes movies about women scholars of religion?!) We realized that in a sense we had written about each other prior to our meeting.

My work as a consultant on the movie, coupled with my research on the cognitive science of media, helped me identify how certain media techniques influence religious belief and belief in the supernatural. I published my updated research in the *Journal of the American Academy of Religion*, describing some of these techniques and their effects.[5] That work coincided with the beginning of my research into UFO phenomena. I quickly realized that the phenomenon offers the best example of how these techniques, the mechanisms of belief, work to inform and sustain religious belief and practice.

Two such techniques are the "based on true events" strategy and something I term the "realist montage." The first is employed in many fictional adaptations of historical events. Historical movies about religion begin with a preexisting assumption that the events to be portrayed are real, as in movies about Jesus and his life. Jesus was a historical figure, and so viewers perceive movies about his life as historical accounts. Of course, they are not. Jesus is usually shown as a white European, yet he was not. Mary Magdalene, one of Jesus's followers, is portrayed as a reformed prostitute, although there is no evidence that she was a prostitute, reformed or otherwise.

The second strategy, realist montage, splices different scenes together to create a narrative and establish a cognitive connection between them. Scenes from fiction are placed side by side with scenes from real life, or nonfiction, to create a realistic effect. This method is often used when pictures of scenes that originally had no causal relationship are grafted together to form a new meaning or a new narrative, as well as to create internet memes (Figure 4.1).

This technique is used to great effect in the closing scenes and credits of *The Conjuring*. The movie was based on the lives of Ed and Lorraine Warren, as well as the Perron family, all of whom are real people. Their pictures and their real names, as well as pictures from their lives, were placed alongside pictures of the actors (in costume) who had played them. This created an effect whereby the spectator could easily conflate the real lives with their fictional portrayals.

Another way to generate belief in a fictional production or a fictional adaptation of historical events is to get cultural authorities to comment on the piece in the media. When the marketing company Grace Hill Media was promoting the blockbuster movie *The Passion of the Christ* (2004), they invited scholars of religion and theologians to a prescreening. When these authority figures published their reviews, it created a buzz in the media. I realized that I functioned as

FIGURE 4.1. Behind-the-scenes photo of Vera Farmiga and Lorraine Warren from *The Conjuring*. Source: MovieStillsDB.com.

such a cultural authority for *The Conjuring*, when the director James Wan tweeted that they had hired a consultant for the movie.

Neuroscientist Jeffrey Zacks helps us understand how movies about presumed historical or real events create the conditions in which spectators can easily conflate fiction with fact. We create cognitive models of events, Zacks explains. These models can get conflated, especially if two or more events resemble each other—even if one is real and one is fictional. "It's not the case that you have one bucket into which you drop all the real-life events, another for movie events, and a third for events in novels," he notes.[6] The tendency to confuse fact and fiction—to put a model into the "wrong" bucket—is elevated when fictional movies use techniques that create a sense of realism, like the realist montage and the "based on real events" strategy.

Such use of the mechanisms of belief is inherent in documentaries and in propaganda. Zacks looks at Alfred Hitchcock's *Saboteur*, a film about a Nazi saboteur who is supported by American sympathizers. He argues that although the film was fictional, the producers had a real-world agenda—they wanted to alert Americans to the fact that such events could happen. As happened years later with the marketing of *The Passion of the Christ*, cultural authorities commented on *Saboteur* in the media and lauded it as accurate on many levels, if not literally true (as it clearly wasn't). Zacks notes:

> I would bet that for many viewers the events of the film were integrated with the information they got from the newspapers and newsreels. If you were to have come back a couple months after the movie was shown and ask viewers about a factory bombing, I would bet a good number would tell you about the factory bombing without realizing they were describing fiction. That is just what makes such a movie effective as propaganda: If viewers integrate models of events in the film with their models of events in the world, then they will use the events in the film as the basis for modifying their behavior in the future.[7]

The problem with fictional representations that are accepted as real or conflated with the real is that it happens unconsciously. Perhaps people can be trained to control this process, but probably not. Zacks does suggest strategies to combat it. He cites a study in which students were shown a factually inaccurate film about historical events. The researchers tried to combat this effect with "a very specific warning that the movie might contain bogus information, and correcting students when they initially accepted the bogus facts. Those two interventions reduced the effect of the misinformation."[8] But it didn't remove the effect completely. Another problem is that producers most likely will resist putting such disclaimers on their movies or media productions, because the confusion between fact and fiction has proven to be very lucrative.

The issue is much larger than just the virtues (or evils) of catering to commodity capitalism. Immersive virtual reality and the infrastructure that supports it are the real game-changers in this story. Arriving at conclusions similar to Zacks's, scholars at Stanford University's Virtual Human Interaction Lab have found that "the brain often fails to differentiate between virtual experiences and real ones."[9] This fact, coupled with new, digitally inspired media techniques that mimic the strategies traditionally employed by Hollywood producers, means that we can now generate a truly immersive experience of what has heretofore been unreal and impossible. The inability of spectators to separate the film version from the factual version of events, and the blending together of fictional productions and real-life events work together to create something entirely different and new—even new belief systems. In fact, it has helped generate the belief system of the UFO.

IF *STAR WARS* WERE REAL IT WOULD LOOK LIKE THIS

Scott Browne is right. A new era is upon us, the era of the fabricated UFO, which is also the object of near-universal belief. The fabricated UFO is the best example of how the mechanisms of belief—realist montage, the potential reality of an event, the reliance on cultural authorities, the splicing of digital characters into iconic historical photographs, and depictions of scenes from ordinary lives—work together to create belief. From the 1990s series *The X-Files* to the contemporary digital productions that combine computer-generated imagery (CGI) with real, historical footage of military combat from World Wars I and II, these productions combine and blend fact and fiction, playing coyly with the spectator's desire to know a "truth." It is a perfect storm of belief-generating mechanisms and forces that result in a lucrative industry, all based on faked videos and rumors of truth—and the future-real—which is the potential reality of the UFO.

Belief in UFOs is increasing.[10] UFO-related programming is increasing too, especially within settings that ostensibly offer information about real events, like the National Geographic Channel and the History Channel. Increasingly, this fictionalized programming about UFOs is being interspersed with productions about historical and real events. Brad Dancer, National Geographic's senior vice president for audience and business development, recently acknowledged that companies like his might play a role in bolstering UFO belief. Speaking about National Geographic's recent publicity campaigns, he said, "We were trying to have a little fun and see if pop culture references have had an impact on people's beliefs. Hollywood may have contributed to the belief. As movies portraying aliens become increasingly convincing, they may subconsciously affect people's attitudes."[11] In a poll, National Geographic asked its audience what they believed the world would be like if extraterrestrials were real. Respondents thought that *The X-Files* was the best representation of what actual UFOs and aliens would be like.

The public chose this program for the same reasons that *The X-Files* is exemplary of this trend. The show is an account of a systemic—and systematic—government cover-up of the reality of UFOs and extraterrestrials. Is it fictional? To the extent that there have been such government cover-ups of purported UFO events, it is not. Declassified documents have revealed that several governments, including those of the United States and the United Kingdom, have indeed covered up and managed information about reported UFO events.[12] The 1953 Robertson Panel, which was the impetus for Project Blue Book, suggested a media campaign to manage public perception of the phenomena. Significantly, the report recommends the very kinds of strategies used by the screenwriters of *The Conjuring*, the student producers of *The Blair Witch Project*, and Grace Hill Media's marketers—that is, the use of documentary-style techniques and authoritative experts to help mold public perceptions.[13]

The X-Files mimics real life in a way that is much more powerful than *The Conjuring*, partly due to the fact that *The X-Files* was a weekly television series that ran for almost ten years (1993–2002). The loglines of *The X-Files* invited spectators to consider that "The Truth Is Out There" and, more important, that it was okay to admit "I Want to Believe." This latter logline, juxtaposed with the image of a flying saucer, became one of the most popular memes of the 1990s and 2000s. The memes incorporate a fundamental belief that there is other intelligent life in the universe with a concomitant recognition of doubt, thus brilliantly preserving the potential believers' credibility and sidestepping the issue recognized by Jung: that no sensible person would admit to belief in UFOs. Belief in the *possibility* of extraterrestrial life, however, is another thing altogether. Apparently, that belief seems much more sensible.

Video and media productions about UFOs use techniques that foster belief by creating *realistic-appearing* images and scenarios, in the very sense that Zacks warned about and that Brad Dancer referenced when he said that "movies portraying aliens" are becoming increasingly convincing. *How could that be?* An alien has never been found that we know of, so how could production companies make a product that is *convincing*? And just who is being convinced?

A clue to the ways in which audiences are being convinced to believe in UFOs lies in a newish media genre called *specialist factual programming.*[14] Its focus is on making factual or historical events "special" with the help of digital technologies. The mechanisms of fostering belief, such as realist montage and "based on real events" taglines, are very evident in their products. The very name, "specialist factual," is full of irony, as Philip K. Dick uses a similar term in his 1966 short story "I Can Remember It for You Wholesale," which inspired the *Total Recall* movie franchises. The evil company in Dick's story produces "extra-factual memory," implanting virtual memories in people. Did the person who coined the name of this new genre read Dick's short story? In any case, many contemporary production companies have units devoted to specialist factual programming. The genre, by design, uses the very techniques that foster the mixing of the real and the unreal. It is appropriate to wonder how human memory is affected by these kinds of productions.

The production company known as Impossible Factual focuses exclusively on specialist factual productions, using digital technologies to recreate historical events. They claim to have "broken new ground in Specialist Factual programming, science, history and drama documentaries."[15] Their clients include National Geographic, the History Channel, and the Smithsonian, all of which are known to produce historical and other presumably factual programing. One of their products, a documentary-style film, splices digitized (and Photoshopped) extraterrestrials into the very fabric of world history. What is the fabric of world history? The pictures and narratives that we use to remember it.

In the movie *The Great Martian War 1913–1917,* Impossible Factual uses realist montage to simulate World War I, creating a war with an alien race that (obviously) never really happened. The movie took social media and television by storm. Tellingly, the company describes its film as a documentary, a designation usually reserved for factual productions. In the overview the production company mimics the tone used in descriptions of films about real-life events:

> A world-wide catastrophic conflict fought 100 years ago between humankind and a savage race of extraterrestrial invaders. A cast of modern-day historians and aging veterans tell the story supported by a fusion of historical archive and dazzling special effects. This unique allegorical tale of the horror of war is a tribute to the real-world events of World War One.

The producers offer the disclaimer that the film is an "allegory," but they also rank it with other, more factual work: "Last year he [the CEO] originated a 90 minute fake documentary/drama telling the story of the Martian Invasion of 1913 and a Four-part series about World War One for History US." This side-by-side placement (realist montage) establishes a relationship between these two things, one factual and the other fictional. The relationship is solidified by an image in which the two are captioned in a similar way: *WWII's Greatest Raids: TV Series Documentary* and *The Great Martin War 1913–1917: 2013 TV Movie Documentary.*

How must the viewer interpret these images, so seamlessly presented, side by side? We *know* it is not real, but Zacks's research shows that our brains process the information and then categorize these productions as equally realistic. And what about young audience members, some of whom believe in the survival of the extinct prehistoric shark Magaledon because they have seen it portrayed in specialist factual programming? How do they interpret the company's promotional pitch for *The Great Martian Invasion?*

UFOs and extraterrestrial scenarios lend themselves to "fictionalized factual" productions for many reasons. They've become a part of our lives through television programs like *Star Trek,* movies like *Star Wars,* and a host of others that came before and after these iconic American productions. Cultural authorities like spokespersons from NASA make regular announcements about potential non-human life in the universe (albeit microbial or bacterial), thus lending credibility to the existence of extraterrestrials. Digital technology, utilizing techniques like realist montage, place extraterrestrials within images of ordinary life, thus naturalizing their presence. *The Great Martian War 1913–1917* is just one among innumerable digital efforts to insert UFOs, aliens, and galactic visitors into real cultural histories. In my research, I came across so many examples of this development that I am willing to label it a trend. The trend is both "top down," in that companies like Sky Cinema have produced short videos that insert *Star Wars* characters into ordinary life, and "bottom up," as private citizens have created websites and other productions that do the same. The result is that there are a slew of videos and other visual media of extraterrestrials that live side by side with our most familiar and important historical events—and within the fabric of our ordinary lives.

One of the best examples of this trend can be found on the popular website *If Star Wars Was Real* (ISWWR). The website features iconic photographs of well-known events such as the assassination of John F. Kennedy and the explosion of the Hindenburg blimp. Characters from *Star Wars*, such as the robot R2D2 and stormtroopers, are expertly introduced into the photos to look as if they were present when these events happened. It is at first quite difficult to pick out the alien characters because they look so natural and are so expertly Photoshopped into the American landscapes.

The creator of ISWWR's tongue-in-cheek mission solicits others to embark on a journey to reveal a hidden history. He wryly invokes the potential realism of the project and asks others to help in the mission of locating the lost "real" photographs of the characters from *Star Wars*:

> If you're a Star Wars fan, you probably, often think of it and discuss it with your friends as if Star Wars was real. So much information exists on planets, species, technology and the force, that it might as well be! In fact, you may know more about Star Wars than you do about the "real world." We all know what a creative genius George Lucas was as a story teller, and we also know of his passion for history, which caused us to ask the question: "How much of Star Wars is influenced by real events in the past?" To answer this question we began contacting historians, libraries and archives all over the world and were surprised to find that many of them actually knew of

photographs or documents that could definitely be the "ancestors" of objects and/or creatures in the Star Wars universe. However, in each case the evidence seemed to have disappeared sometime in the early 1970s. As we continued to probe into this further more and more national archives in several countries closed their doors to our investigation. Then individuals started coming forward with personal items such as, photographs, artifacts, even old currency that gave us evidence that, not only was Star Wars influenced by history, some of it may actually be *real!* This website endeavors to catalog and display any proof we can find that Star Wars is real. If you have evidence of this amazing fact, please share it with us. Though national archives around the world are choosing to keep it quiet, you can help us expose this global secret and add to the phenomena that is Star Wars.[16]

I reached out to the creator of ISWWR. He wanted me to know that he was fully aware that *Star Wars* is not real, and that the characters are fictional. He did not want me to write that those participating in the quest to "uncover" the lost *Star Wars* photos believed it was true in any way. I assured him that I wouldn't, as I believe him and I also believe that the people who make the specialist factual productions are aware of the distinction between what is real and what is virtually real. That was not the focus of my interest in his project, in any case. My point is that researchers find that our brains process visual and digital imagery in a different way from what we suppose. Exposure to films and media that mimic real life fosters belief and can impact memory.

In another example of the "*Star Wars* in ordinary life" trend, photographer Thomas Dagg created a project he called "Star Wars" in which he recreated the scenes of his youth, with the addition of characters from *Star Wars*. He explains how he imagines his childhood: "If it was a blizzard outside I always thought of Hoth. If I saw a jogger I would imagine them with Yoda on their back like Luke Skywalker. That was my childhood." Dagg was surprised by the popularity of his project: "Since it was such a personal project I didn't expect it to blow up, but it's been crazy how many other people have identified with it."[17] Dagg, twenty-four, relates that it was *Star Wars* that motivated him to become an artist.

Yet another example is a short video that mimics the genre of the Russian dash cam videos, a popular form of voyeuristic entertainment. Usually, these videos record car crashes in snowy conditions on slippery highways. The stormtrooper version opens like a typical dash cam video. The viewer sees that the car is fast approaching a crash. But the crash does not involve a car or truck. Instead, a stormtrooper stands on the side of the road next to his crashed imperial TIE fighter; if you blink, you will miss it. But it was there. The video, which lasts only thirty seconds, boasts over two million views. The credits on the video link it to Lucasfilm, and it's possible that it was created as advertising for the *Star Wars* franchise.

Videos featuring *Star Wars* characters spliced into ordinary life are so popular that they have generated a new, grassroots genre. One of the best examples is "Death Star over San Francisco," created by Michael Horn.[18] The video, which has over three and a half million views, shows various objects from the *Star Wars* franchise in ordinary scenes in San Francisco. The Death Star hovers over one of the street demonstrations that are common in San Francisco. People play on the beach as TIE fighters hover nearby. All of this looks quite ordinary, and none of the citizens take notice.

The realism of the video has attracted a lot of attention, including an interview with Horn in *Wired*. "Lucas has not called me yet," Horn says, "but if he did, I'd certainly express my gratitude toward him for making my childhood so magical. His cultural and technological legacy is enormous. My favorite Star Wars films are the original trilogy, and of the newer trilogy, I'd oddly have to say Phantom Menace was my favorite."[19]

Early in my research I interviewed a computer programmer who was working on *Oculus Rift*, an immersive virtual reality program contained in a headset, which was subsequently sold to Facebook. Due to the nature of his work, he requested anonymity. He was filled with excitement about the potential of the project—he said that he was working on a revolution. One thing he said struck me as very significant; it had to do with his experience working in the headset environments:

> I work hard and I'm in the set (the IVR set) for a good portion of the day. Sometimes I remember things and then I realize that what I've remembered is not real. It happened in the set, or maybe it never happened. This experience feels like a déjà vu, but what's scary to me is that I am not really sure, was it a memory of something that really happened, or, did it happen in the set? I just can't remember.[20]

I do not take these productions to be metaphors. They are real-life examples that reveal how fictional characters from *Star Wars*, as well as other intergalactic objects like UFOs and extraterrestrials, exist as realities that inhabit our childhood and adult memories and inform our future behaviors. They are cultural realities, infused with meaning and emotion.

A NEW FORM OF RELIGION

As a professor of religion, I am often asked to present my research to community groups. On one occasion, I gave a presentation on the interpretation of aerial phenomena in several religious traditions. There were about fifty people in attendance. Toward the end, I mentioned the religion Jediism, which is inspired by the *Star Wars* franchise. Usually when I speak of Jediism, people laugh, and this occasion was no different. For the record, I do not laugh at any religious tradition. After the presentation was over I was approached by a man and his son. He waited until the people around me dispersed, and then he told me that he was a practitioner of one of the religious traditions I had mentioned.

"Buddhism?" I asked.

"No."

"Christianity?"

"No."

I then immediately knew he was a Jedi, and I felt bad the audience had laughed when I had mentioned his religious tradition.

"You are a Jedi!" I exclaimed.

He smiled proudly. He was a Jedi Knight.

Star Wars characters not only inhabit our virtual landscape but also have inspired a religious movement. In 2002, I became aware that a group of people had claimed *Star Wars* as their religion on a census in the United Kingdom, as a joke. I used this as an example to show my students that defining religion is not easy, but I was certain that it wouldn't be relevant in another year. Yet this event, along with other, independent developments, soon became part of a movement that endured, and now there are official religious groups that claim *Star Wars* as their sacred "scripture."[21] Critics claim that it is not a *real* religion because it is based on a movie. Religions generally propose truth claims regarding a transcendent, or supernatural, element. Movies do not. Yet thousands of practitioners of Jediism believe that there is a transcendent and supernatural element within *Star Wars*— the Force. Of course, the Force is only one of many themes in *Star Wars* movies, but practitioners of Jediism reserve unique autonomy for the Force, apart from its fictional status.

According to Jedi practitioners, George Lucas based the movies on religious philosophies including Daoism and Zen Buddhism. Because these are considered religions, and *Star Wars* is based on and illustrates them, it should therefore be considered a type of scripture that, like a finger pointing to the moon, refers to eternal and transcendent truths. Thus, practitioners of Jediism place their fiction-based religion within a category reserved for traditional religions.

David Chidester, Carole Cusack, and Markus Alteena Davidsen have all studied new religious movements based on movies, science fiction, and other nontraditional inspirations. According to Chidester, "fakelore or fake religion, although invented, mobilized, and deployed by frauds, can produce real effects in the real world."[22] In a more generous vein, Cusack argues, "Studying religions that openly advertise their invention not only enriches what we know about traditional religions, but sheds light on how science fiction speculations and new technologies inform religious belief and practice."[23] She also notes that invented religions illustrate and challenge common assumptions of traditional religions, such as the idea that real entities, like gods or angels, intervene in human affairs. Davidsen proposes a new category of religion. Unlike historical religions, which are inspired by historical events and claim to refer to the real world, fiction-based religions "draw their main inspiration from fictional narratives that do not claim to refer to the actual world, but create a fictional world of their own."[24]

My interpretation is somewhat different. Jediism exists within a milieu of beliefs and practices about extraterrestrials, galactic visitors, and UFOs that posits their realism, if not as a contemporary reality, then as a future one. They are as real to some people as gods, Jesus, and the various Buddhas. Confidence in their existence is bolstered by cultural authorities like NASA's chief scientist Ellen Stofan, who announced, "There will be strong indications of alien life within a decade and definite evidence of it within 20 to 30 years. We know where to look. We know how to look. In most cases, we have the technology, and we're on a path to implementing it."[25] Many UFO-based religions profess the belief that these alien "entities" have left us artifacts; indeed, such "artifacts" inspire Tyler and James to create their innovative technologies. Jediism and other belief systems about extraterrestrials and UFOs are so powerful because they replace, supplant, or even, as in Eddy's case, supplement and revise traditional religious beliefs. They incorporate the realism of historical religions and project it into the future. A basic tenet of these belief systems is that we will find nonhuman life elsewhere in the universe. It is only a matter of time. What's more, these ideas are supercharged because this potential nonhuman intelligent life exists in our world and in our universe, not in a past of questionable historical veracity and not in a nonmaterial postdeath reality.

The context that makes this new form of religiosity possible is digital. Historian of religion Robert Orsi challenged scholars to understand the roles of gods and sacred entities, like saints, as autonomous agents.[26] These examples of how *Star Wars* characters inhabit the ordinary lives of millions of people offer a clue to an answer. We live within a media-saturated world where fictionalized factual productions like those created by Impossible Factual are beamed through screens into the brains of viewers and become real memories that are integrated into the cultural and social imaginary, as well as into viewers' bodies, because a brain is a body. We cannot understand this development within the conceptual frameworks of the real and the unreal, or the humans and the gods, or even the body and the mind. We must understand it at its source—from within the screen itself.

IMAGINATION EXTERIORIZED

Seeing is believing, we say. Yet, at least since Plato, philosophers have shown that the "seeing and believing" construct is deceptive. This idea is known as external world skepticism: we cannot assume that what we see or identify with our senses is real.[27] But the issue becomes much more complicated when what one sees is processed as real, even if it isn't real in the conventional sense. Reflecting on a talk by "alien abductee" Whitley Strieber about the experiences that informed his best-selling novel, *Communion*, Jeffrey Kripal notes the role played by popular culture: "One evening he [Whitley] explained to us that he was perfectly aware that his visionary experience of the visitors was deeply informed by the bad sci-fi B movies that he had seen in such numbers as a kid in the cold war 1950s in southern Texas."[28]

Whitley's consumption of Hollywood's B movies occurred many years ago. Things have changed a lot since then. We don't have to imagine how this experience has changed. We just have to flip open our laptops or engage our telephones—or even just consult our memories—to recognize (re-cognize) the reality. It's as if our imaginations have become exterior to ourselves, existing out there in our media, and our media then determines what is in our heads. Where does the spectator end and the screened media event begin? Where do we draw these boundaries? As Andy Clark has observed in his research into extended cognition, the assumption that cognition is brain-bound, or that it just occurs within the skull, is wrong. Cognition occurs within a network that extends into the environment.[29]

The modern binary of "human" and "machine" is shown to be the real fake, not new religious forms, populated as they are with nonhuman persons and intelligences. Technology scholar N. Katherine Hayles argues that humans coevolve with their technologies.[30] She uses the term "technogenesis" to refer to this relationship. Technologies are not exterior to humans, she says, but as we use them, invent them, and incorporate them as media and biotechnologies, we merge with them in an ever more complicated and inextricable relationship. Some have speculated that this is part of an evolutionary process of the human species, and will impact longevity and the human ability to travel off the planet. Humans—*Homo sapiens sapiens*—will evolve into a different kind of posthuman being. Philosopher Susan Schneider has written that if humans eventually do encounter nonhuman intelligence, that intelligence would be in a postbiological form—a form of artificial intelligence (AI)—because this is the form that "the most advanced alien civilization" would take.[31] This makes sense. Already we biological humans have sent our own AI, the Rover, to Mars to explore the red planet.

The relevance of Robert Ager's analysis of the monolith in *2001: A Space Odyssey*, and his conclusion that the monolith is a metaphor for the cinema screen, seems inescapable in light of research into cognition in media and memory. Ager's observation suggests that Kubrick was even more of a genius than previously thought, as he somehow knew, perhaps intuitively if not consciously, that cinema and its spectators exist in an inextricable and intimate relationship. Ager notes, "After the release of *2001*, Stanley Kubrick openly stated that he created a film that was intended to bypass the conscious rationalizations of its audience and sink straight into the unconscious."[32] Several scenes in the movie focus on the eye, either the artificial eyes of computers and machines or the eyes of the characters in the movie. The cinema screen–human eye relationship is especially well illustrated in the "stargate scene," in which astronaut David Bowman approaches the planet Jupiter, where a monolith has been identified. The monolith represents nonhuman intelligence. As Bowman approaches, the object floats toward him and then morphs into "the stargate," which appears as a screen with brilliant and colorful flashing lights. Bowman's own eye morphs to reflect these lights, and it becomes difficult to distinguish between the stargate and the astronaut's own retina. The boundaries between the spectator and the monolith (as colorful screen) have been erased, or are indistinguishable.

At the end of Arthur C. Clarke's book, in the hotel room where Bowman eventually finds himself, there is a television above the bed. In the movie, the television is replaced by the monolith. The monolith is in front of the bed, where one cannot help but look into it. Ager notes that in the book, the reference to the idea that Bowman himself is living within a movie is explicit: "His feeling that he was inside a movie set was almost literally true." This point is made clear in the movie: just before Bowman transforms into the starchild, the audience sees the actual movie camera crew reflected in his helmet. In these scenes, Kubrick illustrates the imperceptible influence of cinema.

After Ager cracked the code of the monolith and posted his analysis on YouTube in 2007, he received hundreds of thousands of positive responses. Apparently, the time had at last come to understand the movie—and the monolith. Oddly, at about the same time, a series of ads appeared on YouTube featuring key scenes from *2001* with the iPhone superimposed on the monolith. The ads were popular, and there is now a proliferation of videos that feature the monolith and other scenes from the movie in conjunction with various Apple products, some of them authorized by Apple and others produced as entertainment by fans. At least in popular culture, where it matters most, the truth about the monolith has been revealed: there is a human–monolith continuum, the boundaries of which are very vague (Figure 4.2).

There is a dark side to the monolith. This towering obsidian object appears in key scenes in which humans experience an evolutionary shift, as in its first appearance, where it helps a group of hominids by somehow teaching them how to use a tool—a bone. In a later scene, a hominid throws the bone into the air and it travels into space to become a satellite. The bone, which, used as a weapon, enabled one group of hominids to dominate another, is now a satellite, and the cinematic association of the two suggests that the latter is a modern tool of dominance. Interestingly, in one of the later Apple ads, this entire scene takes place on the screen of an

FIGURE 4.2. Monolith presaging the iPhone, from *2001: A Space Odyssey*. Source: MovieStillsDB.com.

iPhone. Perhaps the "dominance" association between the bone, the satellite, and the iPhone in the ad is unintentional. Perhaps it reflects a truth.

There are other dark elements in the movie, one of which is a program funded by the Department of Defense in which subjects are treated with hypnosis, drugs, and special effects to make them believe that they are in contact with alien intelligences. The Department of Defense program is part of a public relations effort by which the government hopes to acclimate humans to the reality of extraterrestrials. This minor scene in the movie provides an interesting framework for interpreting the cultural development of the alien abduction phenomenon, which has rested on the idea that humans can access suppressed memories through hypnotic regression. The entire premise of John Mack's book *Abduction: Human Encounters with Aliens* relies on his ability to uncover others' memories of alien abductions through hypnosis. I have encountered several such experiences in my own work, reported by people who had not been hypnotized, but this tradition does need to be reassessed given what is now known about how media technologies influence how humans think and what they remember.

David Halperin, a scholar of the Merkabah, the Jewish mystical tradition that arises from the visionary aspects of Ezekiel's wheel, has written extensively about the UFO phenomenon.[33] Halperin has examined the case of Betty and Barney Hill, whose alien abduction narrative was the first to be popularized in the media. It may also have been the first time hypnosis was used on people who claimed to have been abducted by aliens. This established a precedent that would become a convention for alien abductees. The literature, both supporting and debunking the Hills' experience, is extensive, and a lot of it focuses on their hypnosis sessions. What if what they remembered was not real but virtually real? For the record, I am not discounting the possibility that Betty and Barney had a real experience, but I am placing their experience within a new framework that considers the cognitive science of media.

THE HILL CASE, MEDIA, AND MEMORY

Betty Hill and Barney Hill, an interracial couple, were both active in the civil rights movement. They lived in New Hampshire. On September 19, 1961, they were driving on a rural road in that state, when they spotted a light that resembled a falling star but moved differently. They stopped and used binoculars to try to identify it, but then got back into their car and continued their journey. The star, however, continued to be visible and in fact seemed to hover in the sky above them. At one point, it came toward their vehicle, almost filling the windshield with its light. Frightened, they stopped the car, and Barney got out with a pistol he was carrying. Then they returned home and tried to sleep.

Two days later, Betty called the nearby Pease Air Force Base. It was another day before Major Paul W. Henderson returned the call. Betty described the details of what they had seen, but she did not mention the presence of beings or extraterrestrials. The Air Force file says that Henderson explained the sighting as a probable misidentified planet.

After Betty made her report to the Air Force base, she went to the local library and checked out a book about UFOs by Donald Keyhoe, a retired Marine aviator who was head of the National Investigations Committee on Aerial Phenomena, a civilian research organization. This was Betty's "book encounter." In the book Keyhoe contends that there are alien beings that are more technologically advanced than humans and that the US Department of Defense is keeping the evidence secret. As Betty and Barney recovered from their experience, Betty believed that more had happened than they had at first surmised. Additionally, Barney had been experiencing headaches and nightmares since the event. Betty sought out a qualified hypnotist. In hypnotic regression, the hypnotist would uncover memories of an abduction event. Betty and Barney related, while hypnotized, that they believed that alien beings had abducted them, taken them aboard a UFO craft, and then examined them.

David Halperin's analysis of the Hill incident is relevant in that he highlights its link to the popular media of the time:

> In hypnotic regression on February 22, Barney described the eyes of one of the UFO beings as "slanted . . . [b]ut not like a

Chinese." In a sketch he made under hypnosis, the eyes look indefinably sinister, malevolent: the irises and pupils, not distinguished from each other, are close together, while the rest of the eyes trail away upward, toward the sides of the being's head. Barney later told [author] John Fuller that the eyes continued around to the sides of their heads, so that it appeared that they could see several degrees beyond the lateral extent of our vision.[34]

In 1994, UFO skeptic and pop-culture expert Martin Kottmeyer announced a startling discovery. These "wrap-around eyes," as they'd come to be known in UFO parlance, had been seen by the nation's television audience on February 10, 1964—twelve days before Barney's hypnotic session—in an episode of the science fiction series *The Outer Limits*. The alien in an episode titled "The Bellero Shield" had the same sort of eyes. In other respects as well, the TV alien seemed to resemble the UFO pilots as Barney described them.[35]

In 1991, not long after a flurry of works about alien abductions had been published by Mack, New York City artist Budd Hopkins, and others, the practice of hypnotic regression came under scrutiny. A book called *The Hundredth Monkey and Other Paradigms of the Paranormal* collected skeptical essays about "fringe science." Several chapters focused on UFOs and alien abductions. The authors of the essays included scientific luminaries such as Isaac Asimov and Carl Sagan. One chapter used the then-current scholarship on hypnotic regression to call into question the possibility of retrieving accurate memories of anything. Citing the work of Elizabeth Loftus, Robert Baker wrote:

Many people walk around daily with heads full of fake memories. There have also been a number of clinical and experimental demonstrations of the creation of pseudo-memories that have subsequently come to be believed as veridical. Hilgard (1981) implanted a false memory of an experience of a bank robbery that never occurred. His subject found the experience so vivid that he was able to select from a series of photographs a picture of the man he thought had committed the robbery.[36]

Elizabeth Loftus's research revealed that memory is not like a video camera that dispassionately records what happens. Instead, it is a dynamic process more akin to the way knowledge is generated and preserved in our digital age. "Our memories are reconstructive," she writes. "It's a little like a Wikipedia page, you can change it, but so can other people."[37] Today, we must add that other things can also change it—like a movie or a video game. Maybe the human being is like a Wikipedia page, and we are not the sole editors of our own pages.

The *Hundredth Monkey* was part of a backlash against the alien abduction cultural narrative, but hypnotic regression has persisted as a convention of alien abduction investigations. As scholars of film studies have begun to work with scholars of memory, the results may shed light on hypnotic regression and alien abduction. A recent edition of the journal *Memory Studies* was devoted to scholarship on memory and film. The editors write: "Over the past two decades, the relationship between cinema and memory has been the object of increasing academic attention, with growing interest in film and cinema repositories for representing, shaping, (re)creating or indexing forms of individual and collective memories."[38]

The issue devotes a section to Alison Landsberg's idea of prosthetic memory, that is, memories that do not come from a person's lived experience. The focus is on the "cinema, in particular, as an institution which makes available images for mass consumption [and] has long been aware of its ability to generate experiences and to install memories of them— memories which become experiences that film consumers both possess and feel possessed by."[39] What this means in the case of alien abductions is that when people access their memories, they are accessing both features of an experience and what they have seen that is similar to this experience--which is often movies about extraterrestrials. I am not discounting the possibility that there is a real experience, but the experience is remembered with and through the vast corpus of media products about abductions and UFOs.

As Impossible Factual and other specialist factual production companies create documentaries that target young audiences and splice extraterrestrials into visuals of real historical events, the cultural memory of these events will change. How it will change remains to be seen, but there are indications. The Jedi I met recently is a sign of how religious forms change over time and across material conditions. For the most part, potential abductees and their hypnotists no doubt proceed with the honorable intention of trying to access real memories of an event. Unfortunately, this isn't always true of other players in the alien abduction game field, who seek to commodify these narratives in the interest of commercial gain.

David Halperin looks at the case of the Walt Disney Studios' 1995 *Alien Encounters from Tomorrow Land*, which was a television program and a theme park exhibit. Now defunct, it featured the testimonies of real alien abductees, carefully edited by the producers. (Apparently, some of the testimonies included explicit references to sex with aliens that never made it into the program or the theme park.) The producers used "experts" like artist Budd Hopkins, who used hypnotic regression to access memories of abductions, and included footage of military bases, thus lending the project an air of credibility. The program and park deployed many of the mechanisms and techniques that help foster belief, including employing the genre of the documentary, prompting Halperin to remark that it stank "of dishonesty and manipulation."[40] A closer examination of the production reveals what Halperin was writing about.

The documentary opens with narration: "Intelligent life from distant galaxies is now attempting to make open contact with the human race, and tonight we will show you the evidence."[41] That evidence is presented via the mechanisms of belief—that is, formal techniques that lack real-world substance. Michael Eisner, CEO of the Walt Disney Company, is featured in a realist montage. Standing within what looks like a military base, he says:

> In a top secret military installation somewhere in the United States, there are those who believe that the government is hiding the remains of an alien spacecraft that mysteriously crashed to Earth. But more and more scientific evidence . . . reveals that the idea of creatures from another planet might not be as far-fetched as we once thought.[42]

The film then displays newspaper clippings, including one of former president Jimmy Carter's testimony about his own sighting of an unidentified aerial object, as the voiceover cites scientific evidence for ongoing alien visitations. It even shows pictures of what appear to be cells mutating, the implication being that aliens are working with humans at the level of genetic engineering. The film also airs what it calls "compelling footage of home videos" of what look like balloons—the type that Scott Browne identified in his research.

The most disturbing aspect of the production—and what probably most provoked Halperin's wrath—was its insistence that many Americans would likely experience alien abduction in the next five years and that they could prepare for, even acclimate to, this inevitability by visiting the exhibit and ride at Disneyland. The ride, called "ExtraTERRORestrial Alien Encounter," was produced by Disney "imagineers." It is a vivid illustration of how the mechanisms of belief can be adapted to a corporeal-virtual experience. As spectators' bodies are transported through the "ride," they are treated to experts displaying evidence of alien encounters, some of which terrified the youngest participants: as Budd Hopkins shows children cards featuring aliens, they scream and hug their parents in terror. Halperin notes that Hopkins calls this "moving." Something said by one of the ride participants relates to what I heard from the computer programmer who is involved in creating immersive virtual environments and who sometimes has a hard time judging real memories from virtual ones: *"I THOUGHT I DREAMT ABOUT GOING ON THE EXTRATERRORESTRIAL RIDE, BUT IT WAS REAL AND IT WAS TERRIFYING. I'M HAVING FLASHBACKS!"*[43]

Things like this contribute to belief in fabricated UFO phenomena. They influence memory. In a context in which people have a hard time distinguishing credible sources from "fake news," the implications are disturbing. A 2015–2016 study by the Stanford History Education Group looked at the online reasoning of youth about civics and "the ability to judge the credibility of information that floods young people's smartphones, tablets, and computers."[44] The researchers studied middle school, high school, and college-level young people. Many of the participants were unable to distinguish between sponsored content and content supported by legitimate sources. "The students displayed a 'stunning and dismaying consistency' in their responses," the researchers wrote, "getting duped again and again"—and this despite the fact that the investigators weren't looking for high-level analysis of data, just a "reasonable bar" of distinguishing fake accounts from real ones, activist groups from neutral sources, and paid ads from articles. "Many assume that because young people are fluent in social media they are equally savvy about what they find there," the researchers wrote. "Our work shows the opposite."[45]

I recalled a story that Tyler had told me about his own involvement with the media.

"Right before a shuttle launch, I told a prominent news reporter that his story reminded me of Scooby Doo and that it's not very accurate. He told me, 'That's OK. I only have three minutes.'

"I told him to give me an hour, and we could make that three minutes much more profound and better. He wasn't interested.

"You can bring them to water and even stick their heads into the water, but you can't force them to drink. It's like they don't want to know and would rather go thirsty.

"They say they do it because the public wants it served up that way, or the public is not that bright, or there's not enough time—but it's bigger than that. It's a deep flaw in the way things are presented to the public, and no one wants to change or fix it."

Research from disciplines as diverse as cognitive science, history, and film studies reveals what Stanley Kubrick knew intuitively: media technologies are not external to our bodies or minds, but inhabit them in specific ways. Kubrick's visionary science fiction has proven to be a reality—not when it comes to space travel, but when it comes to foreseeing the screen as a type of conduit to consciousness.

THE MATERIAL CODE

From the Disembodied Soul to the Materiality of Quantum Information

[The phenomenon] has *a technological basis*. But we cannot ignore the fact that the emotions it generates in the witnesses are religious in nature.

—JACQUES VALLEE[1]

Everything works, in my opinion, as if the phenomenon were the product of a *technology* that followed well-defined rules and patterns, though fantastic by ordinary human standards. Its impact in shaping man's long-term creativity and unconscious impulses is probably enormous.

—JACQUES VALLEE[2]

DRIVING BACK FROM BIG SUR to San Francisco, Jacques Vallee, Robbie Graham, and I stopped for lunch at a dock-side restaurant in Santa Cruz. The sun sparkled on the waves, the day was gorgeous, and I was enjoying the coastline and the salty air. As we sat and gazed at the view, I realized that the restaurant was serving as a debriefing station. For the past week, we had been immersed in a small, intensive seminar with people who studied UFO phenomena and religious events associated with the paranormal. There had even been a sighting of a UFO while we were there, although none of us had seen it. A small group of sky-watchers, sitting on the rocky rim of the Pacific Ocean, had spotted a bright, shiny, starlike object dancing about in the sky on the night of our arrival. Jacques and I interviewed one of the people who saw and photographed the object. He had recently been through a life transformation and he interpreted the sighting as confirmation that he was on the right path.

After lunch Jacques drove me to meet my brother in San Francisco. When he dropped me off, he gifted me with several of his books, one of which was *The Invisible College: What a Group of Scientists Has Discovered About UFO Influence on the Human Race*. The invisible college, Jacques wrote, was J. Allen Hynek's name for a small group of researchers, scientists, and academics who studied the phenomenon under the cover of anonymity. Hynek, an academic and an astronomer himself, in the 1970s was the scientific consultant to the US Air Force program to study UFOs, called Project Blue Book. The term "invisible college" harked back to the scientists who affiliated with Robert Boyle in the early 1700s, at a time when science was considered a suspect and potentially demonic practice. The group is thought to have been a precursor to the Royal Society of London, the oldest established scientific institution in Europe.

In my brother's car, I opened the book. Jacques had signed and dated it: October 2014. The copyright page showed that it was originally published in 1975 and had been reissued in July 2014. I was struck by the last paragraph of Jacques's preface to the 2014 edition: "Because these questions are as open today as they were in 1975, we have decided to reprint this book and to place these burning issues before a new generation of interested readers." The book I held in my hands was a key, though I didn't know it at the time.

It was three years later, after my trip to New Mexico, after my work with Tyler and James, that the realization dawned on me. Jacques's early work, which brought research on the proto-Internet together with remote viewing and extraordinary mind–body states, clarified a new framework for understanding the technologically sacred. On the one hand, the emergence of the internet and cyberspace spawned a lexicon that used sacred and spiritual terminology.[3] Some computer coders even imagined that human consciousness could be downloaded into a nonbiological container, like a computer, and become unfettered, free, and even immortal.[4] On the other hand, Jacques's work was unique in that he highlighted how the UFO was associated with the sacred, but he also suggested that it worked like technology. His early work revealed that UFO events function like contemporary artificial intelligence, "under the radar," and almost invisibly—as in the case of contemporary social bots.

Jacques's concept of the UFO event as a technology is a recurrent theme in his work. For Jacques, secrecy and camouflage are integral to the efficacy and persistence of this technological phenomenon, in much the same way as technologies like social bots effect cultural change, that is, completely under the radar of consciousness. That is where it is most effective, and judging by the life and technologies produced by invisible people like Tyler, I finally understand how this is so.

A COMPUTER SCIENTIST
DOES RELIGIOUS STUDIES
IN THE 1970S

The Invisible College is replete with allusions to Catholic history and culture. The issues he focuses on are in fact the very issues I focused on in my own work on Catholic history, before I had ever considered UFOs. I researched and wrote about the history of the metaphysics of purgatory. Purgatory is a Catholic doctrine that was defined in the thirteenth century. It refers to a state where souls go that are not perfect enough to get into heaven. In purgatory, souls undergo a process of purification that will eventually allow them to enter heaven.

In the twelfth and thirteenth centuries, philosopher-theologians (known as scholastics) debated whether purgatory was an actual place or was more spiritual and purely immaterial. Respected witnesses reported seeing souls from purgatory and testified to physical traces left by them, like burn marks on tables. How could immaterial things like souls leave material traces? The scholastics had recently discovered the works of Aristotle and had begun to apply his dualistic ideas to their own theologies. They were working out what would later become the philosophical position called mind–body dualism, the belief that the mind or spirit is separate from the body and is immaterial.

Jacques identified the very same conundrum with respect to the phenomenon. He wrote, "The UFO phenomenon is a direct challenge to this arbitrary dichotomy between physical reality and spiritual reality."[5] He advocates that researchers throw out the dichotomy because it skews the data. Within ufology, there have arisen two main schools of thought. One emphasizes material issues, and the other addresses subjective and spiritual issues. The materialist school focuses on the empirical effects of UFOs, like radiation burns on material objects or on people, blips on radars, and sightings. This school focuses on "the nuts and bolts" of the UFO event. The other school arose with the advent of the application of hypnotic regression to experiencers and with the contactee and abduction movements; it focuses on the experiencers themselves and the content of the extraterrestrial messages. This bifurcation in UFO historiography was not only a property of the two schools, whose members were sometimes openly antagonistic, but also a characteristic of the UFO report itself.

In his field research, Jacques found that people tended to report different things depending on to whom they were speaking. This happened in the case of Betty and Barney Hill. They reported empirical evidence to the Air Force, the sighting of the starlike object. But when describing their experience to people they felt would not be inclined to scoff, like Donald Keyhoe and later their therapist (who, ironically, did not believe in UFOs), they divulged the story of the encounter with nonhuman beings. Jacques noted that this pattern was repeated so often that "when scientists and the military discuss UFOs, they are not talking about the same part of the phenomenon the public perceives."[6] In other words, there are two datasets, one of which consists of empirical and material effects, the other of which comprises the psychic or subjective aspects of the phenomenon. What keeps these two datasets separate—one secret, the other told to authorities—is the fear of public ridicule, or worse, the loss of one's job or credibility. The "absurd" keeps the phenomenon hidden and on the margin of legitimate sociality.

A similar dual tradition is found within Catholic historiography. Devotional Catholicism is often interpreted as in conflict with, or less important than, doctrinal forms of Catholicism. Devotional Catholicism is associated with popular practices such as prayer to the Virgin Mary or the Sacred Heart of Jesus, and saying the Rosary. An individual's religious experience is impossible to verify objectively. Personal testimonies of apparitions of Mary or Jesus are usually met with disbelief and suspicion on the part of Church authorities. The testimonies of the witnesses, and even the witnesses themselves, become the focus of efforts to verify the reports. If the witnesses are well-respected members of the community, this helps; others will then take the experience more seriously. This emphasis on the trustworthiness of the witness is a prominent feature within Catholic devotional traditions, just as it is within the tradition of UFO reports. This bifurcation within Catholic historiography is also called "private revelation" as distinguished from "public revelation." Private revelation is associated with devotional Catholicism and Catholics are not obligated to believe in it, whereas public revelation is defined as scriptural revelation, in which Catholics are obligated to believe.

The "nuts and bolts" school of UFO researchers believe that given time, and dependent on their complete disavowal of the psychic, weird, and subjective components of the events, mainstream science will embrace their findings. Yet this may never happen—at least, it will not happen soon. The reasons for this are hinted at in Jacques's book, where he wrote that the subterranean and hidden nature of the UFO phenomenon is part of its logic. He proposed that something revolutionary was afoot, using the history of Christianity as an analogy. Early Christianity began as a subterranean belief system, a fringe belief that circulated among various populations and was even actively suppressed by the elites of the era. "This counterculture was *too absurd* to retain the attention of a reader of Plato."[7] Yet this counterculture (or countercultures, as Christian communities in the first century were diverse) was vindicated when Christianity erupted into a state religion, eventually enjoying its current status with billions of practitioners, many of them elites. This is the logic of camouflage. It is sneaky, and time is on its side.

What were the mechanisms by which the subterranean forms of Christianity took root and eventually supplanted Roman imperial theology? How did it maintain its relative dominance over two thousand years? Two drivers are important, the first being media technologies, or forms of socially mediated communication like art and iconography, then the printing press, and finally modern mass media.[8] Additionally, the messages of early Christianity appealed to slaves, women, and noncitizens of the Roman Empire. The Apostle Paul taught that Jesus had brought a message of salvation for all people, regardless of gender or social position. This was a countercultural belief system. It seeped into various subcultures of Rome until it exploded triumphantly into Rome's state religion, Roman Catholicism, which literally means Roman universalism.

This message of salvation for all people had to appear absurd to the Roman ruling class. Certainly, the fact that Christians "ate" their god was scandalous to the Romans, who called Christians cannibals. When I remind my students that receiving communion entails "eating" Jesus, they are usually horrified. They've become acclimated to the absurd. But the absurd is what kept the Christian message from being visible to the Roman ruling classes, while its other countercultural messages appealed to the disenfranchised. This element of the absurd, Jacques points out, is part of the logic of the UFO phenomenon:

> Contact between human percipients and the UFO phenom-
> enon occurs under conditions controlled by the latter. Its char-
> acteristic feature is a constant factor of absurdity that leads to
> a rejection of the story by the upper layers of the target society
> and an absorption at a deep unconscious level of the symbols
> conveyed by the encounter.[9]

The absurd keeps many potential researchers from studying UFO events. Two former students accompanied me to a meeting with a well-known experiencer. In every way, the experiencer's story was a textbook case of a UFO sighting. He was a credible witness in that he was a businessman, and a pilot, and was well known in his community. One day when out fishing he saw a series of aerial phenomena. As a pilot, he knew they were not aircraft. By the time I got to know him, he had told his story repeatedly on television and at conferences. My students were riveted by his testimony—right up until he described flying past the planet Mars on the astral plane and seeing Bigfoot. I recall my students' stricken faces as they looked to me for guidance. Their lips formed silent questions: *Should we believe this guy?* At that point I had become so accustomed to the absurd within both UFO testimonies and Catholic devotional history that such claims didn't faze me. The logic of religion is not rational, although it does form patterns. But that doesn't mean it doesn't have real-world effects or that it doesn't proceed by an internal logic, which is what Vallee has argued. I told my students that I would explain the absurdity later that day.

Within some religious traditions, including Chan or Zen Buddhism, the absurd is intentionally cultivated to an extreme degree. Zen masters or advanced practitioners pose koans, or short, nonsensible anecdotes, to lead their students to experience an "enlightenment" or satori, a mystical experience that is one of the goals of the religion. "What is the sound of one hand clapping?" is perhaps the best-known koan. It doesn't have an answer, and that is the point. The koan fatigues the rational mind, which eventually shuts down to allow for an experience of enlightenment. Jacques wonders if the absurd elements of the UFO event could be like a koan: something that allows humans to attain a state of mind quite different from that which characterizes normal consciousness. Could the UFO phenomenon be a mass koan, working on millions of people, not just a few?

The logic of camouflage works partly because the element of the absurd keeps what is camouflaged underground and hidden, and the absurdity of UFO testimonies ensures that they are not studied in any official or public capacity. What academic would touch the topic of Bigfoot on Mars? George Hansen has written about the absurdity of UFO events in his book *The Trickster and the Paranormal*. He argues that a trickster element of absurdity is inherent to the paranormal and the supernatural, including UFOs. His central theme is that "psi, the paranormal, and the supernatural are fundamentally linked to destructuring, change, transition, disorder, marginality, the ephemeral, fluidity, ambiguity, and blurring of boundaries. In contrast, the phenomena are repressed or excluded with order, structure, routine, stasis, regularity, precision, rigidity, and clear demarcation."[10] He links the proliferation of practices and beliefs associated with the paranormal to cultural revolutions or instability.

When entire cultures undergo profound change, there is often an upsurge of interest in the paranormal. During the breakup of the former U.S.S.R. there was an explosion of paranormal activity throughout Eastern Europe. Healers and psychics featured prominently in the media. This should not have been a surprise because anthropologists have shown that the supernatural has figured in thousands of cultural revitalization movements.[11]

Similarly, historian William A. Christian has linked apparitions of the Virgin Mary to Spanish and European revolutions and social and political upheavals.[12] The paranormal, provocative, and subterranean all come together in Jacques's analysis of the apparitions of the Virgin Mary.

APPARITIONS OF THE BLESSED VIRGIN MARY: THE BEST EXAMPLE OF THE TECHNOLOGICAL ASPECTS OF THE UFO EVENT

Jacques's most elaborate example of the technological patterns associated with the phenomenon is not a UFO event at all, but an event from religious history. For millions and maybe billions of Catholics, the apparitions of the Virgin Mary in Fatima, Portugal; in Lourdes, France; and on the hill of Mount Tepeyac in Mexico are formative to their faith. At these locations, the Virgin Mary has "appeared" at various times, mostly to children. The apparitions attract the attention of local communities, and as word spreads to other villages and towns and eventually to other countries, these locations become sites of hierophany—places where the sacred touches down upon Earth. Apparitions of the Virgin Mary are a convention of Catholic devotional culture, and the mere mention of an apparition will attract crowds of believers and skeptics. The convention, as a spiritual genre, is so well known among the general population that it has spawned parodies and even major films.

In *The Invisible College*, Jacques rereads several of the original sources about the apparitions that occurred in Fatima and Lourdes and places these within a tradition that includes modern UFO events. In other words, he performs a "biblical–UFO" interpretation, somewhat like Eddy W.'s interpretation of the Bible, quoted earlier. Jacques's interpretation, however, is different in important ways. Jacques is not claiming that the apparitions are UFO events or, conversely, that modern UFO events are apparitions. He ceases to define what they are, and instead breaks them down into their constitutive parts, noting their patterns, which he then graphs. He places these data points side by side in a table that he calls a "Morphology of Miracles." Later in the book, he does suggest a conclusion, but it is not what one expects. He doesn't argue that these are visitations from a being that a culture once called the Virgin Mary and that moderns now call extraterrestrial. Instead, he suggests an analysis based on social effects, identifying both apparitions and UFOs as manifestations of a single control mechanism that works like a schedule of reinforcement. In psychology, "scheduled reinforcements" influence behavior by means of rewards or punishments. A well-known example of a reinforcement schedule is the case of Ivan Pavlov's dogs, who learned to salivate when they heard a bell and were given a treat. The salivation response was cultivated through the process of reward and association.

THE EVENT IN FATIMA, PORTUGAL

Within Catholic devotional culture, one of the most important events in the history of the faith is the appearance of the mother of Jesus, the Virgin Mary, to three poor children in Fatima, Portugal, in 1917. The apparition has received the official sanction of the Catholic Church, and several popes have expressed open devotion to "Our Lady of Fatima," as she is called. Pope John Paul II believed the lady saved him from death when there was an attempt on his life on May 13, 1981. May 13 was when the lady first appeared to the three young children, and the pope was doubtless aware of the date. He later put the bullet that almost killed him into the crown of a statue of Our Lady of Fatima.

The apparition was not a one-time event, but recurred over a series of weeks. It started with the three children, nine-year-old Lucia Santos and her cousins, Jacinta and Francisco Marto, who saw an angel in the spring of 1917. This angel appeared to them on three occasions and told them to follow a protocol of fasting and penance. On May 13, and again on June 13, the children saw a beautiful lady. The lady was expected to appear again on August 13, but the local parish priest had become so concerned about the growing publicity the sightings were generating that he held the children in jail on that day. By that time crowds of people had begun showing up to experience the apparitions.

The children reported seeing the apparition six times in all. The culminating event was the "Miracle of the Sun," witnessed by thousands of people, including avowed skeptics, on October 13, 1917. The Portuguese media covered the event and captured the phenomena with photographs.

Although the story of Fatima is known by almost all Catholics, and even to millions of non-Catholics, Jacques notes that the actual events are mostly unknown and have been changed through media and over time. Few people realize

> that the entire sequence of observations of an entity thought to be the Holy Virgin had begun two years previously with a fairly classical sequence of UFO sightings. . . . The B.V.M. [Blessed Virgin Mary] may dress in golden robes and smile radiantly to children, but the technology which "she" uses is indistinguishable from that of gods and goddesses of other tongues and garb; it is also indistinguishable from the technology surrounding the UFO phenomenon.[13]

The technology includes recurring images (Jung would say archetypes) and elements, including the arrival of a shining being in a small sphere (much like the spheres described by Alison Kruse), spinning aerial discs, humming noises, heat effects, healing phenomena, some people witnessing it while others do not (as when Eddy W. saw the saucers and his wife did not), and the message of the beings, which seems absurd and often includes the injunction to remain silent (here, the secrets of Fatima).

Months before the apparitions of the Virgin, Lucia was out walking on a hillside when she saw a shining cloud descend from the sky. In the cloud was the outline of a human form. She saw this again on a subsequent walk. Then one day when she and her cousins were out playing, a white light passed over them and the humanlike being appeared again. This time she was clearly observable as a shining youth. She gave the children instructions. They were to pray and do penance. The experience left the children physically enervated for hours; as noted by Jacques, this is a pattern in UFO contact events. The request that the children perform prayers and penances reminded me of Tyler's protocol of practices that he believes help him connect with his beings.

The records of the children's testimonies indicate that they identified the lady just as "a lady," not as the Virgin Mary, although the entity had said that she was from heaven. She first appeared to the children in an oval of bright light, and she instructed them to return to the same place every month, where she would greet them. They did so, and as rumors of the events spread, crowds swelled to thousands. Although only the children could see the lady, others reported seeing a cloud descend when the lady was supposed to appear and ascend when she disappeared. They also reported hearing a buzzing sound when the lady was supposedly speaking to the children. Journalist Maria de Freitas interviewed an eyewitness:

> "Lucia jumped up and exclaimed 'Oh Jacinta, *there she comes already, there was the lightning*,' and then ran to kneel at the foot of the oak.
>
> "And did you not see anything?" de Freitas asked.
>
> "Me? No ma'am. And no one boasted about seeing the lightning. We would follow the children and kneel in the middle of the field. Lucia would raise her hands and say 'You bade me come here, what do you wish of me?' *And then could be heard a buzzing sound that seemed to be like that of a bee.* I took care to discern whether it was the Lady speaking."
>
> "And everyone heard it?" the reporter asked.
>
> "Well, it could be heard very well!" she answered.[14]

At least thirty thousand and perhaps as many as one hundred thousand people showed up to see the display that the children predicted would happen on May 13, among them skeptics, journalists, and of course believers. The following account was written by Professor José Maria de Almeida Garrett, who was on the faculty at the Sciences of Coimbra, Portugal.

It must have been 1:30 p.m. when there arose, at the exact spot where the children were, a column of smoke, thin, fine and bluish, which extended up to perhaps two meters above their heads, and evaporated at that height. This phenomenon, perfectly visible to the naked eye, lasted for a few seconds.

The sky, which had been overcast all day, suddenly cleared; the rain stopped and it looked as if the sun were about to fill with light the countryside that the wintery morning had made so gloomy. I was looking at the spot of the apparitions in a serene, if cold, expectation of something happening and with diminishing curiosity because a long time had passed without anything to excite my attention.

Suddenly I heard the uproar of thousands of voices, and I saw the whole multitude spread out in that vast space at my feet . . . turn their backs to that spot where, until then, all their expectations had been focused, and look at the sun on the other side. I turned around, too, toward the point commanding their gaze and I could see the sun, like a very clear disc, with its sharp edge, which gleamed without hurting the sight. It could not be confused with the sun seen through a fog (there was no fog at that moment), for it was neither veiled nor dim. The most astonishing thing was to be able to stare at the solar disc for a long time, brilliant with light and heat, without hurting the eyes or damaging the retina. [During this time], the sun's disc did not remain immobile, it had a giddy motion, [but] not like the twinkling of a star in all its brilliance for it spun round upon itself in a mad whirl.

During the solar phenomenon, which I have just described, there were also changes of color in the atmosphere. Looking at the sun, I noticed that everything was becoming darkened. I looked first at the nearest objects and then extended my glance further afield as far as the horizon. I saw everything had assumed an amethyst color.

Then, suddenly, one heard a clamor, a cry of anguish breaking from all the people. The sun, whirling wildly, seemed all at once to loosen itself from the firmament and, blood red, advance threateningly upon the earth as if to crush us with its huge and fiery weight. The sensation during those moments was truly terrible.

All the phenomena which I have described were observed by me in a calm and serene state of mind without any emotional disturbance. It is for others to interpret and explain them. Finally, I must declare that never, before or after October 13 [1917], have I observed similar atmospheric or solar phenomena.[15]

Different people reported seeing different things, yet all were convinced that they had witnessed something entirely supernatural. The church, after thirteen years of investigation, approved the event as worthy of belief, albeit under the category of "private revelation," as distinguished from "public revelation," which is something Catholics are obligated to believe:

The phenomenon, which no astronomical observatory registered and which therefore was not natural, was witnessed by persons of all categories and of all social classes, believers and unbelievers, journalists of the principal Portuguese newspapers and even by persons some miles away. Facts which annul any explanation of collective illusion.[16]

Even without the church's endorsement, the Fatima apparitions would have a deep influence on the imaginations and real lives of Catholics. One of the predictions of the lady was that Jacinta and Francisco would die before they reached adulthood, which sadly proved true. Lucia entered the Order of Carmelites as a nun and would live as a cloistered member of the convent until her death in 2005.

In his close readings of the apparitions, Jacques's strategy is to attend as much as possible to the first order of events as they transpired, keeping to the original language used by the experiencers, whom he calls *percipients*. He ignores the second-order, evaluative interpretations of the entity as being the Virgin Mary. He takes the same approach to UFO events. He refuses to believe or disbelieve, for example, that Betty and Barney Hill received messages from extraterrestrials from the star system of Zeta Reticuli, which is what they claimed. He does not, however, dismiss the experiences as not having been real. He borrows his methodology from anthropologist Cynthia Nelson, who studied apparitions of the Virgin Mary in Zeitoun, Egypt. "As phenomenologists," Nelson writes, "we suspend judgment as to whether the apparition is *really real* (a question for scientific naturalism) and attempt rather to understand what people do when confronting stress. If men define situations as real they are real in their consequences."[17]

This makes it possible to analyze the social effects of the phenomenon without being distracted by the content of the experiences. This method helped Jacques discover that if one graphs the occurrence of UFO flaps, which are multiple sightings over time, the graph appears to suggest a schedule of reinforcement.[18] Jacques is not committed to the conclusion suggested by the graph, but offers it as a speculation and possible way forward in research. He is, however, committed to the idea that the phenomena appear to be technological.

The idea that contact events like apparitions of the Virgin Mary function in ways similar to technologies was also suggested to me by another innovative scholar long before I had ever met Jacques or had even thought of UFOs. When I was applying to graduate programs, I took the opportunity to interview a professor whose work on technology inspired me. Donna Haraway was known for her work on how human–technological engagement effaces the conventional binaries between humans and technology, humans and animals, animals and technologies, and so forth. Her work presaged feminist technoscience and cyborg epistemologies, or theories of knowledge. I arrived during her office hours, when she was officially available to talk to students, and explained my plan of study. I told her that I wanted to study the then-recent apparitions of the Virgin Mary in Medjugorje, a small town in what was then Yugoslavia, now Bosnia and Herzegovina. I explained that I thought I would use Freudian analysis to understand the phenomenon. After a silence that seemed to last forever, I quickly learned that this was a bad idea. Dr. Haraway asked why I would use a Western European theory to analyze another culture's belief system. After another long, seemingly interminable silence, Dr. Haraway offered some guidance. She asked me to think about what was happening internally to the experiencers who were watching the apparitions. I thought about that, and at the time, I had no idea. She then asked another question: What happens to you when you watch a movie? I still didn't understand the point she was trying to make, but these questions would later help me understand Jacques's research on the connections between contact events and technologies.[19] Could media technologies, even movies like *2001: A Space Odyssey,* function like apparitions?

2001: A SPACE ODYSSEY REVISITED, AND NETWORK RELIGION'S AUTONOMOUS AGENTS

Toward the end of *The Invisible College,* Jacques outlines a morphology of miracles. He places the elements of apparitions alongside elements of UFO sightings and events. They include the following: humming sounds associated with a sighting; the arrival of a shining disc, globe, or sphere; feelings of enervation after a sighting; sounds like thunder or booms; and unusual clouds. He does not mention, although he could have, the ensuing transformation of personality that often occurs, in which the experiencers feel as if they have a mission and completely rearrange their lives to fulfill it. There is also the "psychic component" that Jacques mentions, which was reported by the children who witnessed the apparition, as well as by St. Teresa of Avila. This component is experienced as a direct knowing of what the beings seem to communicate. It is as if the beings somehow get inside the heads of the experiencers, as if there are no barriers between them.

In the 1970s, Jacques offered technology studies as a possible explanatory framework for these odd events and strange patterns of effects. Subsequent research in the interdisciplinary studies of embedded and extended cognitions has sharpened the frame that Jacques constructed. The work of scientists like Andy Clark helps frame the psychic elements of the percipients' experiences. Clark challenges the conventional assumption that what happens in the mind originates there. He argues that cognition, or thinking, or what's in our heads, is not bounded by the skull. Instead, "cognitive systems may include both non-neural parts of the body and even the beyond-the-body environment."[20] The idea that technologies and other tools can extend human mental capacities is not new; Marshall McLuhan aired this proposition in the 1950s. What is new is the recognition of an autonomy that technologies have achieved or, probably, already had all along. This autonomy is now supercharged by the technologies' ability to program themselves. As I write this, the headlines are abuzz with news that the social media site Facebook shut down two social robots that had created their own language that was unknown to their human creators.[21] Media technologies inhabit human consciousness in ways that have been largely unacknowledged and in ways that are disturbingly autonomous.

This research, supplemented by neuroscientist Zacks's analysis of film's impact on cognition, helps make the connection between events like apparitions and UFO sightings and media technologies. Both movies and sightings are "events" in that they have distinct beginnings and endings. Zacks's research indicates that people cognize some media or film events in ways that are similar to real-life events.[22] Returning again to the example of *2001: A Space Odyssey*, one finds many of the elements of the UFO event. In Clarke's book the monolith is described as exuding a humming noise. When the monolith appears in the opening scenes of the movie, in the soundtrack we hear Richard Strauss's tone poem, *Also Sprach Zarathustra*. It begins with humming and leads into methodic drumming sounds. In each scene in which the monolith appears, so does some form of humming. Technology is a constant feature in the movie, in which the artificial intelligence is named Hal, whose autonomy turns out to be deadly. The climax of the film reveals a baby (possibly) within a shining globe or sphere. The appearance of the baby perhaps signifies the transformation of the main character, astronaut David Bowman. It's all there—the glowing sphere, the humming noises, the strange artifact, and the transformation.

Placed within the context of human–technology networks, the film could certainly function like a mass apparition or UFO sighting. Haraway's question clarified this connection. The movie contains the elements of the UFO event and leverages them better than a real-life event could, reaching millions of people with its visual film experience. But it's not just a virtual experience provided courtesy of celluloid and bytes; it is a real experience. We know that media can bypass the conscious mind and flow straight into the unconscious mind, where it forms memories and occupies its own place. This suggests that the realism of fictional characters and narratives must be re-examined, first as actors within the unconscious but also as potentially real and autonomous agents. The psychic component of UFO and apparitional events once experienced by the few can now be experienced by millions, due to media technologies. The beings really are in our heads; for those born in the 1950s and beyond, these beings first entered our minds when we were children watching shows about UFOs and aliens and continue to live there now that we are adults. As Clark points out, "We should consider the possibility of a vast parallel coalition of more or less influential forces, whose largely self-organizing unfolding makes each of us the thinking beings we are."[23]

N. Katherine Hayles suggests how events and media populated with Jacques's morphology of elements can inhabit our universe. The underlying issues involve the very complex dynamics between deeply layered technologically built environments and human agency in both its conscious and unconscious manifestations. Recent work across a range of fields interested in this relation—neuroscience, psychology, cognitive science, and others—indicates that the unconscious plays a much larger role than had previously been thought in determining goals, setting priorities, and other activities normally associated with consciousness. The "new unconscious," as it is called, responds in flexible and sophisticated ways to the environment while remaining inaccessible to consciousness, a conclusion supported by a wealth of experimental and empirical evidence.[24]

This insight illuminates the role that the "book encounter," and now the "media encounter," plays in the evaluation of anomalous events, from their initial interpretation to their subsequent narrative elaboration into stories, films, urban legends, and lore. Much of this process takes place beyond conscious awareness, so it functions invisibly—that is, it is camouflaged.

Jacques's early work anticipates these developments. His work on ARPANET, the prototype of the internet, occurred within the rich, mind-bending environment of Silicon Valley in the 1970s. He was steeped in information studies, computer science, and studies of remote viewing and telepathy. These studies were not separate. Some of Jacques's early publications focused on the effects of burgeoning new technologies on the human mind and experience. His research on remote viewing within the medium of the internet and what was then called "computer conferencing" was published in several venues.[25] One of the advantages of the internet and computer conferencing, he wrote, was that it provided a way to date and timestamp observations made by separate individuals who were far removed from each other in space and time. In effect, the technology confirmed the impressions and thoughts that people would happen simultaneously.

Vallee also suggested that the human interface with the burgeoning technologies would shift the experience of time and space and reveal a more accurate model of time and space and of consciousness:

> The theory of space and time is a cultural artifact made possible by the invention of graph paper. If we had invented the digital computer before graph paper, we might have a very different theory of information today. . . . What modern computer scientists have realized is that ordering by space and time is the worst possible way to store data. . . . If there is no time dimension as we usually assume there is, we may be traversing incidents by association; modern computers retrieve information associatively. . . . If we live in the associative universe of the software scientist rather than the Cartesian sequential universe of the space-time physicist, then miracles are no longer irrational events . . . at a time when we are beginning to suspect that computer-based network communication may create altered states conducive to psychic functioning.[26]

In other words, experiences that currently appear uncanny and inform religious experience, like synchronicities and powerful, meaning-filled coincidences, would be seen to have been generated by an associative process that worked like a search engine. They would no longer appear to be miraculous because they would be generated through a field of technological–human interface and exchange. One example of this is the social bot–generated synchronicity. I had been working on this phenomenon when I decided to reach out to Jacques and tell him of my findings. My work had thus far been exploratory. I was collecting synchronicities that people had experienced on social media that involved advertisements and social bots. There were so many, and experiencers reported that they were no less powerful than the conventional types of synchronicities that I had encountered in my previous work on Catholic devotional cultures. Jacques alerted me to articles he had written about this topic in the 1970s. Of course, this was prior to the rise of the social bot, and the experiences that involved new technologies had changed since his original research. Jacques had wondered, "Is it possible to promote coincidences and peculiar effects by systematically creating physical [information] structures? Consciousness could be defined as the process by which informational associations are retrieved and traversed."[27] Jacques not only accurately predicted the types of anomalous experiences people would have using digital technologies but also indicated that these experiences would influence theories of consciousness.

I found that the partial answer to his question is "yes." The following example highlights the real effects of "faked" synchronicity on an experiencer. This experiencer is a fan of Jacques and completely understood that his synchronicity experience was "synthetic," as he termed it. Significantly, however, it was no less profoundly meaningful for him because of that:

I was trying to encapsulate my sense that our new internet marketing mechanisms have duplicated the synchronicity engineering that Vallee suggests might be part of the mechanisms of the cosmos allowing interaction/co-creation between mind and everything else. Yesterday morning I had commented on my friend's posting of several Michelin Man/Bibendum images. Then, later that night, as I was looking at a random webpage, I noticed, through the cookie-detecting/Facebook-enabled targeted advert there appeared on the sidebar my new avatar: an advert for Michelin tires featuring Bibendum himself making a "thumbs-up" gesture. It really felt like a significant synch for me at that moment—DESPITE my knowing full well the likely advertising mechanisms operating behind the scenes to make it happen. So basically, a modern technological mechanism that approximates the possibly innate nature of Universe as described by Jacques Vallee as the cosmic bulletin board/associative universe that "reads" our "intentions" or desires to be connected to certain things/information.[28]

Experiences of synchronicities, as Nietzsche pointed out in the nineteenth century, are the engines of religious belief and practice. They function this way for practitioners within UFO cultures as much as they do for members of Catholic cultures. Nietzsche was warning against the easy adoption of the "religious" position regarding them, and he suggested that one instead focus on how the human mind has reached its highest ability, that is, to ascertain the interplay of chance and interpretive skill. In other words, he suggests that rather than leading to a dogmatic religiosity, these experiences should instead lead to a state of wonder about existence. His aphorism ends on a decidedly mystical note:

> We do not want either to think too highly of this dexterity of our wisdom, when the wonderful harmony which results from

playing on our instrument sometimes surprises us too much: a harmony which sounds too well for us to dare to ascribe it to ourselves. In fact, now and then there is one who plays with us—beloved Chance: he leads our hand occasionally, and even the all-wisest Providence could not devise any finer music than that of which our foolish hand is then capable.[29]

For Nietzsche, Chance assumes the role of Providence. Even as he naturalizes the powerful experience of synchronicity, he elevates Chance and highlights the truly uncanny experience that it can produce, an experience so strange that one hesitates to attribute it to human action or causal events. Like David Stinnett, Jacques naturalizes synchronicities. For Jacques in particular, synchronicities reveal the reality that consciousness is based on information:

> If you believe that the universe is a universe of "information," then you should expect coincidences. You should expect, since we are an information machine—that's what our brain is, it's primarily an information machine and consciousness gives us the illusion of a physical world and there is an illusion of time—if this is the case, then you can expect coincidences. It's like putting a keyword into Google or Yahoo!; you put it in and get a lot of relevant information back. That doesn't seem strange to me because that is the way that information has been organized. Maybe the universe is the same way. If it is this way, then coincidences are nothing strange. It is just an indication that this is the way that the universe functions.[30]

Jacques's early work and worldview presaged what would arrive in the 1990s and beyond, the "biotechnical imaginaries" promoted by synthetic biologists of Silicon Valley and their financial backers.[31] Noting that bioengineers affirmed that "life can and should be treated as 'programmable matter,'" scholar Gaymon Bennett writes that the language and assumptions of contemporary synthetic and biotechnologists now appear unsurprising as the success of industries of biotechnologies help their associated ideologies and worldviews become accepted. When bioengineer Drew Endy had "playfully shown that cells could be made to store information in a manner reminiscent of binary code," it appeared that the code of matter had finally been cracked.[32] Life, matter, and bodies did indeed appear, as Jacques suggested, to function like computers. Echoing Hayles and other critics, Bennett writes that the biotechnologists "took information to be fundamentally immaterial."[33] Although this assumption is incorrect, that does not mean that it is wrong to say that matter functions like a code, or like information.

HUMAN SATELLITES AND DNA: THE MATERIALITY OF INFORMATION

Like Jacques, Tyler believes that the phenomenon is technological. He believes that it interfaces with humans directly through biotechnological antennae—cellular functions or even human DNA. In this sense, he assumes, humans are technologies. Tyler does not believe that information is immaterial, but he posits a model of the universe in which information and matter exist at different frequencies.

In the search for extraterrestrial life, humans are the preferred sensors. Tyler said:

> SETI [the Search for Extraterrestrial Intelligence] seems to
> look in all the wrong places with the wrong sensors. I guess
> any search is better than no search but it won't come from a
> laser detector. The best detectors are humans like you and their
> net results and may be certain light frequencies or the study
> of physical relics. The wavelength of optical lasers is unlikely
> to find anything. But it sounds good and can obtain funding.

Tyler believes that human beings are designed to interface with the phenomenon, but only under certain conditions,
and some human beings are better able to "connect" than
others. I knew that Tyler had a unique job, and I learned
that part of the job description was that he was to be placed
in certain locations. Apparently, Tyler's mere presence was
supposed to facilitate certain required events and processes.
His immediate bosses didn't know how this functioned or
happened, yet it was true. The more I learned about what
Tyler did and why, the more I realized that the skills he
possessed weren't normal and were not even spoken of. They
were just acknowledged. They were, in effect, real because
they were useful. I was reminded of my student, José, whose
training as a Marine squad leader included learning about
and using a "sixth sense." He and his team used it because
it worked, not because they believed in it. A similar process
seemed to be involved in Tyler's case. He explained that he
believes not only that the phenomenon is a technology but
also that humans are receptors of the information provided
by the phenomenon, and some humans are more capable of
receiving the signal than others.

In his opinion this was a spiritual process:

> From a Christian religious perspective, humans interface
> with God through the practice of worship and prayer with a

mechanism called the Holy Spirit. My view and philosophy starts with that as my framework. It is further developed than this, though, in that I believe that the human body and mind act like a computer. A computer is the best model for how it all works. It's hard not to see that as a viable model if you study the human anatomy and the processes of life. The human spine when dissected under live conditions looks much like a very elaborate electrical circuit, with color-coded wires as nerves and blood vessels. The first time I observed a long incision for scoliosis surgery, I remember how much the spine, when opened up in surgery, looked much like the electrical panel inside an expensive satellite. You hear scientists speak about our brain as the central processor and our nerves as the motors to our muscles. The power source to the body is our energy, which is obtained from the food we eat, which is created by the energy in sunlight. Some would say our RAM is the prefrontal lobe and our hard drive is housed in our hippocampus and the mother board is likened to our skeleton, which provides the structure to our body. A peripheral might be our arms and legs. The mouse has already become our index finger.

Tyler continued by describing the energetic processes of the human body:

DNA stores biophotonic particles as data where it is transferred through our body very much like optical data in fiber-optic wiring. When human DNA, as a molecule, is stretched out it is about two meters long so that it has a natural frequency of 150 megahertz. DNA also has a code which follows the same logic and rules as human language as it relates [to] syntax, semantics, and grammar. If true, this leads one to assume that we have a programmable body via DNA.

If we assume this model of human physiology, then it's reasonable to think the human body, given its computerlike functions, could act as a transmitter and receiver not much different than our home computers and WiFi systems where the internet source enters our houses either through a hard-wired fiber network or a satellite signal wherein the data is then processed and used within our homes through our routers and radio-frequency signals.

It's interesting that the natural frequency of our DNA is similar to that of the frequency used for satellite communication. Also, taking the computer model a step further, the calcium in our bones and its physical hard structure could act much like a large antenna to aid in sending and receiving data, as well as house many of our DNA and stem cells in the bone marrow. In this model the human body and DNA become a biological internet and the data is likely stored with light photons, which in recent studies indicates an ability for the photon to share an exact twin state without restrictions of time and space. In other words, when a force of energy is excited in one photon, its sister photon, thousands of miles away, experiences the same force instantaneously, which is referred to as entanglement.

Tyler's understanding of the body/phenomenon interface as an information translational process is grounded in materiality. The body and materiality are indispensable conditions for this process, he believes. He also refers to the idea that the human brain is not the center for thinking or even for the most important types of thoughts—the kind that lead to innovative and truly creative thinking.

I find that this memory/contact with an intelligent source (God) is much smarter than me, is more creative, and carries more energy and insight than I ever could using my own RAM and hard drive in my simple mind. I need to have access to the depth and wisdom of this God-like internet to reach the fullest potential in my life, it seems.

I practice a protocol of yoga to access my router rather than my RAM, direct sunlight to charge my DNA photonic cells, propagate the natural energy outside in nature, and focus on my core body rather than my brain given that the concentration of our DNA is between our hips and neck. I think humans like to believe the head is the smartest and only part of their intelligent system, but this is probably because it is the location that houses our sensors—eyes, ears, and nose. The body becomes as important as or even more important than our brains to optimize the storage, reception, and transmission of this divine signal. So for people who practice calming the mind to allow the body to become more involved in the "thinking" process and perform functions that stimulate their computer, router, and WiFi signals, it wouldn't be surprising to find out that they are much more creative, productive, and intelligent. They've learned to leverage whatever knowledge is on the internet of the divine universe rather than rely on their small outdated laptop (their personal brain) that has no internet signal.

Bennett says that the synthetic biologists of Silicon Valley and their biotechnological lexicons have become normative—that is, their worldviews are now our worldviews. The cultural worlds of the biotech industries impact and influence millions and perhaps billions of lives. Their beliefs about what is sacred, or beyond human, filter through media technologies and into our own imaginations and memories. The human body is at the center of this sacred interface. The latest generation of scientists understands the materiality

of information. Dr. Nicole Yunger Halpern, quantum physicist and author of the blog *Quantum Frontiers: A Blog by
the Institute for Quantum Information and Matter @ Caltech,*
writes: "I like my quantum information physical."[34] Scientists
like James and Tyler are working to identify just what this
material substance is, and how it works.

THE HUMAN RECEIVER

Matter, Information, Energy . . . Contact

> All family members present were willing to discuss
> what happened with me, all acknowledged hearing an
> external voice urging them to look at the UFO, and all
> of them felt in some way profoundly affected by their
> UFO encounter. This is one example from dozens
> of cases, which I have personally investigated in the
> Canadian province of Ontario, that demonstrates to
> a certain degree of what is known in UFO studies as
> "high strangeness."
>
> —SUSAN DEMETER-ST. CLAIR[1]

"WHILE DRIVING HOME FROM MY parents' home I spoke
to God for the first time. I looked up at the stars and said
to both God and the Entities with which I was interacting,
'I congratulate you—you have managed to completely
transform a total atheist into someone who now believes
in God, the spirit world, and life after death, more than any
Catholic priest in Miami.'" Thus spoke Rey Hernandez,
while driving in his car one day. *What* had happened
to Rey?

A UFO sighting or event often has the effect of completely changing the direction of one's life, much like a religious conversion experience. This was the case with Rey,

a lawyer and self-described rationalist and atheist. After a series of sightings and related paranormal experiences, Rey, together with Apollo astronaut Dr. Edgar Mitchell, Harvard astrophysicist Dr. Rudy Schild, and Australian researcher Mary Rodwell, cofounded the Dr. Edgar Mitchell Foundation for Research into Extraterrestrial Encounters or FREE. It is the first global, multilingual study of people who claim to have had UFO-related contact with non-human intelligence and related paranormal experiences. Rey reminded me that, when I refer to his work, I should mention that he is just one of many qualified researchers "who have put in hundreds, even thousands of hours" in support of the organization.[2]

As Jacques Vallee discovered, there are two types of UFO reports. There are those that are reported to "authorities" and those that are revealed to sympathetic listeners (who are sometimes also authorities). The fear of ridicule keeps many UFO testimonies subterranean, submerged within subcultures that nevertheless grow each year. This chapter explores the experience of Rey Hernandez and his wife, Dulce, and documents the unexpected twists and turns it took once he publicized it.

The Hernandezes' experiences are instructive for several reasons. First, each saw something extraordinary, yet they interpreted it differently. Dulce is a devout Catholic and interpreted her experience as divine and within the framework of Catholic theology. Rey, who was an atheist prior to his experience, is still interpreting it. In his work Rey delves into the testimonies of UFO contact. In its secular form, testimony is a form of evidence. To give testimony in a court of law is to provide information that is supposed to be true and to correspond to real-life matters. If one provides false testimony, it is called perjury. Within the history of religions, testimony is also a type of evidence. Many religious traditions are built upon the testimonies of believers. Believers report extraordinary things and events, such as miracles or sightings of supernatural beings. This testimony is often accompanied by information about the credentials of those who testify. In both religious cultures and UFO cultures, the "credible witness" is an important feature that helps lend credibility, if not to the actual reality of extraordinary claims, at least to the fact that credible people experience extraordinary events.

Many of the scientist-believers I interviewed think that the phenomenon functions like a technology, and that the human is a receiver and transmitter of information. Rey and his cadre of colleagues—twelve retired physicists, neuroscientists, psychologists, and scientists—employ various methods, including quantum physics, to explain the relationship between consciousness and contact with non-human intelligence. For them, this interaction defies a dualist construction of spirit and matter and bridges the rift between two camps of researchers in ufology: the "nuts and bolts" materialists and the subjectivists, those who focus on the testimonies of experiencers. According to Rey, the scientists associated with FREE are working on theories that will provide an explanation of how these experiences are both physical and subjective: "This new holographic theory challenges us to deconstruct the artificial wall of separation erected between events that occur only in consciousness, and those that can manifest on a physical scale."[3] The key is in the code, and Edgar explains how this is so.

THE SERIES OF EVENTS THAT CHANGED REY

It was very early on a Sunday morning in March of 2012. Rey and Dulce's beloved Niña, a Jack Russell terrier who had been a member of their family for sixteen years, had become paralyzed the night before. Rey had contacted a veterinarian friend, who said that Niña had most probably suffered a cerebral hemorrhage. The friend offered to open his office the following day, Sunday, to euthanize Niña. Deeply saddened, Dulce turned to her faith. She prayed to God that he would send his angels to cure Niña. That morning, her prayers were answered, in a way that would shatter Rey's atheism and confirm Dulce's faith.

Rey, in an interview, relates the first of a series of extraordinary experiences, and figure 6.1 is a depiction of what Rey saw. Rey's wife saw something like figure 6.2.

> My wife woke up and [checked on] the dog to see if she had regained her mobility. Our pet was not able to move at all except just from the neck up. My wife then carried her down the stairs, and when she got down there she saw an object that was floating four feet off the ground, one foot [away from] the wall, and it was metallic in shape—approximately like an upside-down-U. . . . It had these two ring lights in the center. My wife, being the good hardcore Catholic from Mexico that she is, knelt down and started praying . . . basically [saying,] "If you're a bad spirit, leave. But if you are a good spirit or an angel or the Virgin Mary [stay]." Mexicans always see the Virgin Mary everywhere [Rey laughs]. And she said, "Please stay and don't let my dog suffer. My poor Niña." Niña is her name, which means "little girl" in Spanish.

Then all of a sudden these green lights started blinking and started flashing on her—like scanning her. At that point she freaked out and she started yelling for me. She started screaming my name. It was six in the morning, and I thought she had seen a cockroach or a little mouse on the floor [Rey laughs]. I just totally ignored her. After 10 or 15 minutes of screaming for me to come downstairs, she went upstairs and literally hauled me out of bed. When I got downstairs, what I saw was not the object that she had seen. . . . What I saw was, I guess could be described as a plasma-object. This was not just an object; I call it a plasma-being, a light being, because it did control my mind. It was . . . approximately two-to-three-feet in width, one and a half to two feet in height, cylindrical in shape, but it didn't have any external outer edges because it was pure energy plasma. Multicolored, translucent, and when I looked at it I did not have any peripheral vision . . . just straight ahead at that object. I could not see to my right or to the left or up and down. . . . I was just focused only on that object. What I did was quite irrational—I stared at it, I waved my hand at it, and then I said, "Ah B.S." . . . Then I turned around, I walked upstairs, I went to my bed, I folded my hands on my belly, and I looked straight up at the ceiling. So for 15 minutes I was in this hypnotic state with nothing entering my brain/my consciousness. After 15 minutes, it was [as] if the hypnotist said, "OK Kid, wake up, we're finished with your wife and your pet." And all of a sudden I woke up and I said, "Oh my god, what in the world just happened?" I ran downstairs and there was my wife jumping up and down, saying "Hallelujah! Hallelujah! The angels cured her! The angels cured her!" She was running around the living room dancing, and the dog was running up and down with the energy of a little puppy. Right there my whole worldview was totally shattered [Rey laughs]. That was the first event.[4]

FIGURE 6.1. Rey Hernandez's depiction of what he saw, the "red energy being."

FIGURE 6.2. Dulce Hernandez's depiction of what she saw, "the energy craft."

Dulce said that she had not seen what Rey reported seeing. He insisted that he had been asleep for forty-five minutes after he left the living room. He pointed at the clock to demonstrate that forty-five minutes had indeed elapsed. Dulce insisted that she never left the living room and that Rey had never gone back upstairs. According to her, she had walked downstairs with Rey behind, looked down, saw Niña running around, and then started to celebrate. Then she saw Rey. Their recollections of the event were completely different. Later, Rey would incorporate the idea that "missing time" must have been a factor in the event, and that the non-human beings had taken his wife and dog, healed them, and then returned them.

> My wife does not want to speak much about the incident and acts like nothing of consequence happened—to her this entity was merely an Angel that had answered her prayers. Maybe she is correct. Our living room corner wall is on the north-western corner of our house. At 6 am that corner is dark because light does not enter that corner. We have closed drapes on the western window as well and that part was dark because the sun was just rising on the southeastern side. We also have a wall dividing the windows from the sun rising in the east from this western corner. We know what we saw was not an optical illusion.

This event shattered Rey's view of reality. At the time, he said, he was a "pure rationalist":

> I went to Catholic mass but just to comfort my wife. I had never read any UFO, ancient alien, paranormal or "new age" books. I believed that all the new age "metaphysics" litera-ture was pure BS from ex-hippies even though I considered

myself an ex-hippie while living in Berkeley, CA, from 1981 to 1988 while attending a PhD Program in City and Regional Planning. I was a total skeptic. I was a pure rationalist and any "metaphysic" or UFO related themes were pure BS. On that day, my world view came crashing down.[5]

After this experience, Rey did what most experiencers do: he sought out materials to help him understand what had happened to him. He had never had any type of paranormal experience and certainly never encountered an "energy plasma being." He wasn't Catholic like his wife, so he wasn't sure it was an angel, although he wasn't ruling out that possibility either. He thought that he could find answers in the UFO and paranormal literature. Perhaps what they had encountered was some type of nonhuman intelligence. He looked for answers on the internet and ordered "tons" of books about the topic. His intensive "book encounter" was interrupted, however, by more strange and anomalous events.

THE NEXT EVENT

The next event occurred in May of 2012, when Dulce reportedly saw a huge, blimp-sized UFO outside their house with "stained glass windows just like our church" all around the craft. When Dulce later visited Mexico, she claimed to have had a series of additional UFO sightings, some with her family, and saw three eight-foot-tall human-looking beings dressed in white monks' robes floating in front of her.

Rey had his own sightings. The next event provided Rey with more information about the phenomenon and further changed his life and its direction. It was also witnessed by his daughter, he said, and three of his friends. By this time, his wife was having regular sightings of giant UFOs. For her, these were angels and evidence of sacred contacts. She did not tell Rey about these encounters at the time, because she was becoming concerned about his increasingly obsessive interest in UFOs and literature about them.

On August 25, 2012, a few months after the appearance of the "plasma energy being," a friend of the family came by for help with some traffic tickets. Rey decided to wait for him outside. It was around 9:30 p.m. The sky was dark and cloudy and completely devoid of stars. Rey had been learning about UFOs and knew that some people attempt to "call them down." Rey thought, I am going to try this, so he did. Fifteen minutes went by and there were no results. Rey thought to himself, I am freaking losing it; I am going nuts, and he stopped. Just at that moment, he saw an enormous object over his neighbor's roof and backyard.

Rey describes the object as huge, approximately two to three city blocks in length. It was hovering about five feet above his neighbor's house. He saw hundreds of swirling white lights all around it. Then he heard the voice of his daughter, even though she was not present. The voice said, "Daddy, next time you see a UFO please let me know. You and mommy have seen a UFO and I want to see one too." After this, Rey called for his daughter, who was in the house. His daughter, who had just turned ten years old, ran out to see the object, and stared in amazement.

Rey and his daughter gazed at the object for about fifteen minutes, he said, and then his friend drove up with his wife and seventeen-year-old daughter. These people are conservative Catholics and college educated. Like Rey's wife, they attend Sunday Mass and are involved in many different ministries. They weren't interested in anything that had to do with the paranormal, or with UFOs. When they arrived on the scene, Ray says, they were flabbergasted.

"What is that?" his friend asked, alarmed.

According to Rey, they asked repeatedly, "Please tell us what that is."

Finally Rey spoke to them in Spanish: "You know perfectly well what that is."

His friends spent a few minutes discussing what it could be. They thought perhaps it could be strange atmospheric conditions, lights from the cars on the street, or lightning. Rey was not going to tell them that he "called down" this craft. He knew his limits, apparently.

As the speculations of his friends became more elaborate, he decided to try to communicate with the beings, mentally. He told them, "You better come up with something better than this because they don't believe you." Instantaneously, he said, the light patterns of the craft changed.

The craft burst into a spectacular display of hundreds of stars, ten times the size of Venus, that flickered on and off.

Like Carl Jung's friend who reported witnessing, with many others, a UFO in South America and never thought to take a picture of it, the same happened with Rey. He comments on this incomprehensible aspect of the experience:

> After about fifteen minutes of watching this light show of stars bursting all over the place inside the craft, my friends said they had things to take care of and they drove off. Looking back at it I did not even question them leaving. Here they were in the middle of an "event of a lifetime" and in the middle of this they

decided to leave and I did not even question this. This was not rational.

It was the odd reactions of the other experiencers that most struck Rey as unbelievable:

> During our UFO contact encounter, I was fully cognizant and "awake" for almost everything except the realization that we were actually looking and interacting with a UFO craft and its beings. We all had cell phones and yet no one even bothered to take a picture, especially the teenager who always has a cell phone glued to her hands. I also did not notify my neighbor to inform them what was above their house. They were aware of us looking at them because they had turned the light on in their living room and they saw us staring at their house. I also did not run inside to get my video camera or tell my wife. After my daughter told me that there were no mosquitoes outside, I "woke up" and realized that I was under some type of "mind control." I could not understand why I had walked away from a scenario that should have been the front page story of *Time* magazine and every media outlet around the world if I had captured it on video. I quickly got my camera and camcorder and ran outside with both but the huge UFO craft was gone.

Here again is the problem Jung noted long ago. Some UFOs are not photogenic.

Determined not to let such an event go unrecorded again, Rey took the route taken by Alison Kruse. He purchased high-end photographic equipment so he could prove what he had seen:

> I had purchased a large telescope, a night vision CCTV camera with adapters to attach this camera to the telescope, an old used SONY camcorder with the old night vision technology

and a digital camera with high-powered zoom for night shots. I said to myself, "The next time my wife or I see these objects we will be prepared to capture them on video and on camera so no one will doubt us." We know what we saw and they were real. "Next time we are going to prove it."

None of this helped one bit. The phenomenon resisted being photographed by Rey. Yet, it made a lasting impression on him. He has turned inward to assess what it means to be human, a human who lives within an immense universe, and who has a relationship with something like God.

REY'S "DIRECTED" BOOK ENCOUNTER AND THE ENSUING SYNCHRONICITIES

The day after his close contact experience with the huge UFO craft, Rey saw a YouTube video on near-death experiences that discussed the quantum physics of consciousness. He immediately stopped searching the internet and purchasing books about UFOs. Instead, he began to order books on near-death experiences (NDEs) and consciousness studies. Over the next four months he devoured more than two hundred such books, sometimes reading for eighteen hours per day. He was obsessed. He neglected his job and his family, and did not go outside or watch television or use the internet. Instead, until December 21, 2012, he spent all of his time reading.

Dulce became concerned. She doesn't use the internet, she is not interested in UFOs or NDEs or consciousness literature, and she rarely discusses her experiences except to say that they are "her angels." She was concerned by the obsessive nature of Rey's interests.

Significantly, Rey felt as if this intensive book encounter was being orchestrated by the nonhuman intelligence that had been interacting with his family. After four months, he felt that he was being taken to the next level of his education. After his immersion in studies of consciousness and the literature of NDEs, he experienced a powerful set of synchronicities. The synchronicities involved meeting people who had experienced NDEs, and also hearing, for the first time, about his father's NDE. Rey was struck by the timing. What were the odds, he wondered, of meeting people who had experienced NDEs just after he had learned about them for the first time? And what did these have to do with the UFO experiences?

After these events, Dulce told Rey that he needed to believe in God. She said that she knew that people in their church believed in God, but her belief was different from theirs. She said she could *feel* God and her angels. "I can feel God. I feel these spirits in my hands when I pray and I can feel the energy of God and these spirits in my body." Rey didn't accept his wife's Catholic interpretation of these strange events, but he did not reject it.

At this point, Rey was utterly and truly confused. He continued to read, and to be confused by what he read. Then he experienced yet another unusual event. It came in the form of an out-of-body experience that combined visual information and a direct message. After the experience, Rey believed that he had been given a special project—a mission. The mission was to present to humanity the relationship between the nonhuman intelligences that were interacting with him, the spirit world, and the physics of consciousness.

THE DEVELOPMENT OF THE
DR. EDGAR MITCHELL FREE
FOUNDATION

After these events, Rey believes that he was given a mandate by the beings who had been interacting with him.

As he was driving through rush-hour traffic one morning, he had an experience that he describes as a download experience, or an extraterrestrial telegram. He said that he felt like he was inside a large spinning wheel with many spokes. Each of the spokes represented a particular anomalous experience, such as an NDE, a UFO contact, or an out-of-body experience. He later called these "contact modalities," as, he explained, each of them was a way that nonhuman intelligence interacts with humans.

He described how he then received a telepathic message, not via a voice, but via information:

> You need to inform humanity of the relationship between us (the nonhuman intelligence), the spirit world (the reality we transition to after our death), and consciousness (the physical structure of our cosmology). You will need help. There are two criteria for this help: this is not about making money and there has to be minimal ego.

After this he experienced another series of powerful synchronicities. He relates that after his first experience he had sent emails to ten well-known researchers in the field, one of whom was Mary Rodwell. Mary is a researcher who claims to have supported over three hundred thousand experiencers, and she has written a number of books about her work. Mary didn't respond to Rey's email until after his rush-hour experience. To Rey, it was a very meaningful communication that occurred directly after he was charged with the mission to found an organization.

Mary introduced Rey to Dr. Rudy Schild, who was interested in UFO contactees, consciousness studies, and quantum physics. Rudy is an emeritus professor of astrophysics at the Harvard-Smithsonian Center for Astrophysics and a retired tenured professor of astrophysics at Harvard University, as well as the editor-in-chief of the *Journal of Cosmology*. Rey was impressed that Rudy was interested in his experiences, and gladly recounted them in a phone call.

> I informed him of my "adventures" including the OBE event that had occurred the day before where I was given information about consciousness and the contact modalities. He was fascinated. He informed me that in fact, the information I received on what I now call the "contact modalities" can all be explained through the quantum hologram theory of physics and consciousness (QHTC), a theory developed by the late Apollo astronaut Dr. Edgar Mitchell.

Rudy suggested that Rey form an organization, and offered to serve as its science adviser. He also provided Rey with the number for Edgar Mitchell, the former astronaut and Rudy's mentor. Rey phoned Edgar and found that they lived very close to one another, so they decided to meet. The meeting proved to be very important for Rey and influenced the creation of the organization that would become FREE.

> When I arrived at Dr. Mitchell's house, we exchanged stories. He told me about his "awakening" in space and his early years growing up in Roswell, New Mexico, the site of the world famous Roswell UFO crash. He told me that he worked at a local

airport when he was a young teen and he was paid via flying lessons. Edgar's parents owned two farm supply stores in the Roswell area and he knew most of the ranchers and workers in the area because they were always in his parents' stores. He told me that after he came back from the moon he was not only a national hero but a hero to the folks in Roswell. When he returned to Roswell, many of the old timers and their children began to pull him aside and told him very intimate stories of the ship that crashed in Roswell. Edgar informed me that based on the information he was given by very reliable individuals, individuals he had known most of his life, that the Roswell crash was real. He then told me about his work as a test pilot for the Navy. He also told me that many of these test pilots were admitted into the NASA program as Astronauts. He even told me of some of the "Experiences" of the astronauts, including Russian Cosmonauts, in space that were similar to his involving a series of paranormal experiences. His stories went on and on for hours.

Like Rudy, Edgar offered to assist Rey in the formation of an organization. Rey replied that he was confused about what the organization would do, but Edgar told him that the answer would come to him, adding, "It always does." After his meeting with Edgar, he spoke to Mary. He asked her if she would help him found the organization with the help of Rudy and Edgar. After a few days of considering the idea, she agreed to help Rey and she came up with the acronym FREE, for the Foundation for Research into Extraterrestrial Encounters. Rey relates, "Thus, FREE was started over a three-day period under the guidance of some unknown non-human intelligence."

According to Rey, there had never been an in-depth academic study of the topic of UFO-related events. Rey proposed that FREE undertake the first comprehensive, multilanguage, quantitative and qualitative data-driven research study of the topic. In my discussions with him about FREE, he was careful to note that FREE is not an organization devoted to ufology. He said, "This paradigm has revealed very little about this phenomenon over the last sixty years. A new paradigm is needed and this is the Consciousness Paradigm."[6] He explained that FREE's mission was to understand the relationship between the science of consciousness and contact with nonhuman intelligence via what he termed "contact modalities." He said that Edgar firmly believed that a study that focused on the experiencer was important, so FREE's motto became "Disclosure from the Bottom Up." Disclosure is a term used by ufologists that means that UFOs have revealed themselves, or that there is a public awareness of their presence.

ESOTERIC COSMONAUT EDGAR MITCHELL: THE FRINGE OF THE FUTURE

Through his association with Rudy and Edgar, Rey forged headlong into the study of quantum physics. Within my growing research circles, which included invisibles and *visibles* such as my academic colleagues, the field of quantum physics was the go-to explanatory framework for impossible skills like remote viewing, information downloads, and the strange physical aspects of UFO events, such as their ability to appear and disappear. Even my atheist colleagues entertained quantum theories as possible explanations for the extraordinary abilities that certain saints were reported to have possessed. A colleague who scoffed at my interest in UFO cultures was nonetheless fascinated by my work on the cases of saints like Teresa of Avila, who was reported to levitate, and other saints who were said to have been in two places at the same time—bilocation. After one such discussion he sent me a note in which he theorized, off the record, about bilocation. He linked it to his own studies of quantum physics.

"The idea of saints being in two places at once is intriguing," he wrote. "Physical laws seem to suggest the impossibility of being in two places at once, but the idea of 'superposition,' in quantum mechanics suggests that atoms and electrons can be in two places at once. Not only that, but these two things seem to remain connected to one another on some level in that they can influence one another. Of course, larger objects have not been observed (scientifically at least) to be in two places at once. And, I thought it interesting, that in the cases of saints, bilocation is chiefly associated with acts of charity."

"Charity?" I asked. That jogged a memory I had of both Rey and Tyler saying that the idea of humility (not ego) seems to be important to their "beings."

"Can you say more about your idea of charity?" I asked.

"Scholastic philosopher Thomas Aquinas views acts of charity as divinely infused/inspired. This would place the saint both in the world and not."

I was mostly a bystander in the discussions of quantum theory and mechanics, but I was intrigued that so many of the scientist-believers used this relatively new branch of physics to explain the phenomenon. This included Edgar, one of six humans to have walked on the moon on the Apollo 14 lunar landing mission. Edgar earned a PhD in aeronautics and astronautics from the Massachusetts Institute of

Technology (MIT). He was also the founder of the Institute of Noetic Sciences (IONS), which is dedicated to the study of consciousness, and Quantrek, an institute populated by physicists and scientists who study energy and consciousness. He founded these institutions after a remarkable, transcendent experience he had while on his way home from the moon, floating in space, and looking at Earth.

> The biggest joy was on the way home. In my cock-pit window, every two minutes, I saw the Earth, the Moon, and the Sun, and the whole 360 degree panorama of the heavens . . . and that was a powerful, overwhelming experience. And suddenly I realized that the molecules of my body and the molecules of the space craft, and the molecules in the body of my partners, were prototyped, manufactured in some ancient generation of stars. And that was an overwhelming sense of oneness and connectedness, it wasn't them and us, it was "that's me," it's all of it, it's one thing. And, it was accompanied by an ecstasy. A sense, "Oh my God, wow, yes!" An insight. An epiphany.[7]

This experience was so profound that it changed the direction of his life. Upon his return to Earth, he went on an extended book encounter, voraciously reading as much as he could on the topic of consciousness. Edgar had been raised as a Southern Baptist and he was a trained scientist, yet he finally found reports of a similar experience within the literature of Hinduism:

> The experience in space was so powerful that when I got back to Earth I started digging into various literatures to try to understand what had happened. I found nothing in science literature but eventually discovered it in the Sanskrit of ancient India. The descriptions of samadhi, Savikalpa samadhi, were

exactly what I felt: it is described as seeing things in their separateness, but experiencing them viscerally as a unity, as oneness, accompanied by ecstasy.[8]

The transition back to Earth was difficult for Edgar, a feeling that Tyler had expressed as well, after each of his launches of satellites and shuttles into space. Tyler said, "It's an intense experience to launch such a big thing into space; the whole crew, the astronauts, the engineers, those in mission control, have to be working together as one unit. Nothing, and I mean nothing, can go wrong. Then, it's such a high when the launch succeeds. Afterward we celebrate. But then, how does a person go back to their normal life? How do we *just* go to the gym? It's surreal in way that is a complete and total let-down. I would call it a form of grief."

I met Edgar on two occasions. I knew that he believed in UFOs and extraterrestrials, so I asked him to meet the small group of researchers that I had organized in California. He would attend our session via Skype. Beforehand I found out everything I could about him and was surprised to learn that, just like the other brilliant scientists I had interviewed, he had been involved with the Stanford Research Institute (SRI). He was also a practitioner of remote viewing. What was more surprising to me was that he had conducted remote viewing experiments in space during the Apollo lunar mission. These experiments were not sanctioned by NASA, and Edgar said that they were "secret." Edgar Mitchell, like Tyler D., was part of the hidden and unofficial history of the American space program that I had been discovering—the cosmonauts and rocket scientists, like Jack Parsons, who believed in extraterrestrial or nonhuman beings that interacted with humans with the goal of helping them achieve space travel and, in

Edgar's case, peace on Earth. (He believes this is a prerequisite for deep space travel.) In a sense, there was a hidden history of esoteric cosmonauts. Edgar certainly fit the bill.

Edgar believed that extraterrestrials or nonhuman intelligences intervened in space launches. Before our Skype session I asked each of the other conference attendees, who were all physically present at the conference, to frame a question to ask Edgar. We would each have time to ask our question and we would all listen to his answers. When it came time to ask the questions, I was the only one who asked Edgar about extraterrestrials, even though that was the theme of the conference. Apparently, the silencing mechanisms Jacques had identified had been strongly internalized by my academic colleagues. Here was an opportunity to quiz an astronaut, a scientist-believer in UFOs, yet most of the questions had to do with whether or not humans would be able to live together peaceably on Earth. This *is* an important question, but it was not the question I would have thought of in these circumstances. And indeed, why would *he* know the answer to that question? He was an astronaut, not a deity!

When my turn came, I thanked him for being a part of our session, and asked my question. "Edgar, I know that you believe in extraterrestrials, and I also know that you believe they have been interfering with our satellites and some of the rockets we launch into space. Can you describe how you came to this knowledge and if you might know why they would be doing this?"

Because of his connections, Edgar said, he was privileged to know that extraterrestrials had dismantled several weapons that the United States had launched into space. He said that they did this because our weapons, particularly nuclear weapons, not only damaged humans and our environment but also somehow damaged their environment. He said that there were different species of aliens, and that there were good ones and bad ones. The ones who intervened in our space explorations were good ones.

I asked him to elaborate, if he would, on the nature of the good and bad extraterrestrials. He appeared happy that I had asked this question. He explained that there are some people on Earth who are in contact with the good extraterrestrials, and that they have missions to accomplish, sometimes in secret. He believed (like Tyler and James) that some extraterrestrials had left advanced technologies that certain scientists can unlock and use for the good of humans and the world. He said that we have already benefited from this technology.

At the end of the interview, which lasted about an hour and a half, I came away with several observations. Edgar used language that I had heard used by many of the invisibles. Certain words and phrases were repeated often enough to form somewhat of a lexicon, or a language group. It reminded me of academics who communicate in their own discipline's jargon, and unfortunately other people cannot understand what they are talking about. I wasn't sure what this meant, other than that there was a group of people who shared a common set of phrases and words and who also shared similar beliefs about extraterrestrials, the US space program, and technology.

Also, Edgar believed that networks of human–extraterrestrial contact already exist. Organizations like SETI, the Search for Extraterrestrial Intelligence, were not the preferred contact centers, apparently. Tyler had mentioned this too. He thought humans, with their DNA and cellular receptors that worked like mini satellites, were the best receivers of contact information from nonhuman intelligences.

According to several of the scientist-believers, including Edgar, quantum physics provides a framework for understanding the paranormal and supernatural events and abilities, including remote viewing, miracles, and contact with nonhuman intelligence. Rey and Edgar each called this the contact modalities. Edgar's theories are elaborated in several of his books, and in his idea of the quantum hologram theory of physics and consciousness. According to this theory, Edgar says, information consists of patterns of energy. Information–energy packets are given off by matter. On some level, all bodies of matter contain information.

Edgar and his associate Rudy Schild helped Rey understand this theory, and Rey published articles arguing that it provides a framework for his contact with nonhuman intelligences. Significantly, he also argued that it retires the conundrum of the subjective versus materialist approaches that has plagued research of UFO events. "I now approach the so-called 'ET contact phenomenon' from a non-traditional perspective, one that embraces both spiritual/psychic and paranormal aspects, as well as decisively physical manifestations."[9]

This theory is able bridge this gap because it posits a reality that is made up of patterns of energy. Edgar's theory is elaborated in his idea of the "dyadic model" of consciousness. This model, according to Edgar, explains how remote viewing, telepathy, and even extraordinary mystical experiences, such as his experience of Samadhi while traveling back from the moon, are possible:

Several factors emerge immediately from considering the mystical experience from the dyadic point of view. The first is that mystical insights are just information that requires interpretation, not absolute and literal realities, that can stand alone. The flaw in cultural interpretation of mystical interpretation is precisely that of interpreting metaphor literally. However, a valid information function is taking place nevertheless. Consider the experience of the nirvikalpa samadhi which is described similarly in different traditions. In this experience the sense of Self merges with the cosmos and reality is experienced as unity of Self with All-That-Is. The experience is accompanied by intense ecstasy, a sense of eternity and a complete loss of fear. The cultural interpretations are generally that the experience represents union with the godhead, or the ground of being. It is the experience of the "peace that passes all understanding." The dyadic model interpretation is that the body/brain is experiencing its "ground state" or resonance with the zero point field. The awareness is the undifferentiated awareness of the primordial field, as the sense of Self is merged totally into the field. The question immediately arises as to why an intense ecstasy plus a sense of security and eternity accompany this state. It is only within the larger question of why nature provided feelings at all that this question may be answered. The internal feeling sense accesses the state of wellbeing of the organism. In addition, the subconscious brain functions integrate information from external senses and from non-local sources to provide a "feeling" of alarm or security as to the state of the environment. The feeling sense also provides reward or punishment for behavior influencing survival: gratification of thirst, hunger, sex drive, and discomfort or pain for dangerous behaviors, etc.

According to Edgar, the feeling of ecstasy indicates that this experience should be repeated. In this way, he integrates an evolutionary component into his model. He explains how this model helps us understand how skills like remote viewing and telepathy are possible:

> Although non-local effects have been observed and studied for over a century by parapsychologists, in the absence of a compelling theory the results have been ignored or disparaged and certainly misrepresented by mainstream science. Non-locality in quantum physics now provides a physical basis for these effects. A large number of investigators for several decades have demonstrated that brain waves can be synchronized and information transferred between individuals across Faraday cage barriers. The results do not obey the inverse square rule of electromagnetic propagation, nor are they time dependent, suggesting the phenomenon is a macro-scale version of quantum non-locality, but with more degrees of freedom than simple particles undergoing a double split experiment.[10]

Edgar worked to establish several organizations devoted to the study of consciousness. He also helped fund and establish the Disclosure Movement, which is a movement initiated by the citizens of various countries to force their governments to declassify documents related to UFOs. Through his connections to astronauts and the US space program, he was able to motivate people who worked for these institutions to testify in front of Congress about UFOs. He is a pioneer who supported scientists who wanted to study consciousness and physics. This is now seen as a legitimate field of study, but when Edgar started out it was not. He has joked that when he began his work on consciousness studies he was called a "space cadet" by some of his colleagues, while others said he had been "lost in space." I place Edgar within a lineage of esoteric cosmonauts and rocket scientists, such as Konstantin Tsiolkovsky, John (Jack) Parsons, Tyler D., and many others—people whose ideas and beliefs might appear to be on the fringe, and are. They may be on the fringe of our future.

Edgar had returned from space with the confidence of one who has been where only twelve humans have ever gone. Several months after my colleagues and I spoke with Edgar, he passed away on the eve of the anniversary of his landing on the moon.

REY REPORTS HIS EXPERIENCE TO THE MUTUAL UFO NETWORK

When individuals with no prior experience of UFOs believe they have had an extraordinary sighting of one, they look for information associated with UFOs to make sense of the event. One of the first things experiencers do after an anomalous sighting is to perform a Google search. They use keywords like "shining object" or "UFO," and inevitably the Mutual UFO Network (MUFON) appears among the search results. MUFON is an organization with the goal of researching UFO-related events scientifically. The organization was founded in 1969 in the midwestern United States and eventually expanded into a national network of units. It is a nonprofit organization that trains "field investigators," that is, people who go on-site to study anomalous reports. The organization and its chapters also host conferences that focus on UFO studies and research. MUFON has been criticized for using "pseudoscientific" methods for investigating sightings, reports, and experiencers, and it has been criticized by experiencers who have input their own reports into its extensive and public database of UFO reports.[11]

I know the North Carolina state director of MUFON and several field investigators. My associations with them have been friendly and professional. Their research methods, on my observation, are completely rational and objective, and err on the side of skepticism. However, individuals associated with MUFON are not necessarily representative. Experiencers I've interviewed say their experiences with the larger organization have not gone well. Several have reported that their experiences have been made public in a completely altered form. When a person reports an experience to MUFON, it goes into a national database of reports, and these reports become the property of MUFON. They can do what they want with them—like sell them to television production companies.

One day Rey received an email from a friend who said that he had seen Rey's family's experience portrayed on the television program *Hangar 1*, produced by the History Channel. Rey was horrified to find that an entire episode was based on his family's experience, but that the events as represented on the show didn't resemble their experience. Disturbingly, the message it conveyed was the opposite of his own and his family's experience. What for them had been a positive encounter was morphed into a terrifying home invasion by extraterrestrials.

Rey saw his own handwriting displayed on the screen. "All the handwriting you saw on the video's pictures was my handwriting; it even had my attorney letterhead blacked out—that is why I know it was my report to MUFON." Rey was understandably upset that his experience, which had changed the direction of his life and which his wife believed was an "angelic" encounter, was portrayed as just the opposite. The miraculous healing of the dog Niña was left out of the episode, as was the fact that Dulce had been praying all night for the healing of her dog. The title of the episode was "UFO Home Invasion."

Rey felt betrayed by the larger organization, but he was generous in stating that the volunteers and field workers associated with MUFON were not at fault. "Many of my dear friends are members of MUFON—all are very nice individuals and I deeply respect them. All of them are volunteers and doing very important and excellent work. My issue is not with MUFON volunteers but with the MUFON *Hangar 1* production. Somehow my field report was not translated to the video because not only were there inaccuracies but there were actual fabrications. I just want to make it clear that the folks that I know that work with MUFON are good friends, highly credible, have done outstanding work, and I fully support them. MUFON is not the issue—the issue is my shock to find out that my story was sold and the fabrications of the MUFON *Hangar 1* production."

Rey asks, "Why the numerous fabrications? I understand it is Hollywood, but why a total fabrication?" At the time the episode aired, Rey had already begun to receive the first round of data compiled by his organization. His dataset included over three thousand reports from people who claimed to have had UFO-related experiences. Overwhelmingly, these experiencers reported positive interactions with nonhuman intelligence.

I have described the mechanisms of belief, which present UFO events as real events that correspond to the truth. The use of a genre associated with truth, the documentary, produced by a company ostensibly related to veridical, historical accounts (in Rey's case the History Channel), supports a central claim of this book—that what one sees on television, in the movies, and on the internet does not necessarily convey the actual stories of those who experience the events. Yet the mechanisms provide a convincing viewing framework. As viewers are entertained by the productions, they are also forming opinions, biases, even memories that help them interpret and form meanings associated with UFOs.

The description of the series as posted on the *Hanger I* History Channel website is painful to read for those who have experienced a UFO event or have knowledge of one:

> There is a place where the truth about UFOs exists; a vast archive of over 70,000 files gathered over nearly half a century. The place is called Hangar 1. Now, it is finally open for investigation. MUFON, an independent organization dedicated to investigating UFOs, has worked diligently to compile, research and store these files. The HISTORY series *Hangar 1* will delve deep into these archives to look for connections, clues and evidence; because only by investigating the files of Hangar 1 can we find the truth about UFOs.[12]

The database that forms the basis for *Hangar 1*'s "based on real events" is filled with the honest reports of thousands of people who have seen, many for the first time, an anomalous aerial object. With good intentions, they report these to MUFON. Where does this data go? In the case of Rey and several other experiencers I have met, they become the basis for consumer products, for entertainment. But the data is also being used by other researchers and organizations. The problem is that a lot of researchers who use it are not the original on-site field researchers. If they were, they could have vetted the original reports. For example, the state director for MUFON in North Carolina rules out all possible explanations. Once she gets a report, she checks with local police and military to ascertain whether there were military exercises or other scheduled aerial events in the area. She also scrutinizes any photographs and physical evidence with the help of trained videographers. If other explanations are ruled out, she grants the report the status of "UFO," that is, "unidentified."

Problems arise when researchers who are not local and who are not trained field researchers take the data and extrapolate to make general statements about the presence of UFOs. Often, aerial phenomena like blimps, drones, and lightning are misidentified as UFOs. These go into the database, along with other reports. Several researchers I have met have blindly taken all of the reports and lumped them under the category of "UFO" sightings. This gives the impression that there are more sightings of truly unknown phenomena than is actually the case. This "big data" approach skews the data.[13]

The truth is potentially "out there," but it's unlikely to be found in media productions.

REAL AND IMAGINARY

Tyler D.'s Spiritual Conversion in Rome

The sky is a neighborhood.

— DAVID GROHL, Foo Fighters

THIS BOOK BEGAN WITH A journey, and it ends with a journey, a plane trip to Rome where I visited the Vatican Secret Archives and the Vatican Observatory in Castel Gandolfo, one of the oldest established observatories in the Western world. For centuries, monks, nuns, and priests peered through telescopes at the starry skies here, nestled next to a volcano and overlooking a startlingly blue volcanic lake.

I was a guest at the observatory and, astonishingly, I was given the keys to their archive, which housed, among many other things, works of Johannes Kepler and Nicolaus Copernicus, revolutionary thinkers who bravely forged the early paths of our current cosmologies. Like Tyler and James, Copernicus was a radical thinker, a person who observed the inexplicable and tried to make sense of it. At one time, the works of Copernicus were banned by the church. Ironically, his books are now prominently displayed in the archive. At the observatory, I felt as if I was in the quiet presence of the hub of unorthodox science, a place where, finally, religion and science did not compete. I was there with Tyler D.

Almost two years had passed since Tyler had taken me and James, blindfolded, to ground zero of the UFO myth in New Mexico. Now, as the culmination of our work together, I took Tyler to Rome, to ground zero of the Catholic faith. Here he experienced a profound religious conversion, right before my eyes. This was perhaps the most miraculous and strange event of my eventful six years of research.

I have made the case that belief in extraterrestrials and UFOs constitutes a new form of religion. Media and popular culture have successfully delivered a UFO mythos to audiences through television series, music and music videos, video games, cartoons, hoaxes, websites, and immersive and mixed reality environments. New research in digital–human interfaces reveals that it doesn't matter what a person might consciously believe, as data delivered through screens shoots straight into memory, which then constructs models of events. On a personal level, many individuals now interpret their own traditional religions through the lens of the UFO hermeneutic.

This chapter will explore a more complicated interpretation of the social effects of contact, where the perceived contact with a nonhuman intelligent, divine being is simultaneously imagined and real. I am not making an ontological claim, that extraterrestrials are real in the sense that couches are real, although they could be. I am arguing that perceived contact has very real effects with powerful social implications.

While in Rome I became reacquainted with a historical figure whom I came to view as a meta-experiencer. Sister Maria of Agreda was a cloistered Spanish nun who lived in the seventeenth century. She was a mystic who wrote books about the Virgin Mary that were very popular in her era and are still widely read. Her earliest works, later burned by nuns of her convent, were cosmographies. They contained descriptions of her astral journeys through space and over the earth, which she recorded as topographies of other countries, cultures, and space. As a young nun, she claimed to bilocate to colonial New Mexico, where she said she met indigenous Americans, taught them about the Catholic faith, and prepared them to be baptized by Franciscan missionaries. The Catholic Church recognizes bilocation as a rare "charism," or sacred skill. A person who bilocates is said to appear to be in two places simultaneously. Maria's story became very popular in the seventeenth century and is even mentioned in textbooks as part of the history of the western United States, where I first encountered it as a student in high school. As I progressed in my research at the Vatican and then in the observatory archive, I was struck by Maria's similarity to Tyler.

THE REASON FOR THE TRIP

I was in Rome to do two things, apparently unrelated. I had agreed to go to the Vatican to help with research on the canonization accounts of a saint and a potential saint. While I was there, I would take the opportunity to assess the historical records of the search for extraterrestrial life—which I assumed I would find in the observatory's archive. The organization that funded my research trip to Rome had asked me to analyze the canonization trial records of St. Joseph of Cupertino and Sister Maria of Agreda. Why was St. Joseph canonized, they wondered, and not Sister Maria? Their stories were somewhat similar and they lived in the same era. Joseph was a seventeenth-century Italian priest who was said to have levitated so frequently that the priests responsible for the case for his canonization stopped counting the number of people who presented themselves as witnesses. There are copious records of the testimonies of his flights, levitations, and even soaring to the ceiling of a cathedral—on at least one occasion taking another person with him. The large number suggests that they were probably not making these stories up. They may have been, but seemingly *something* had happened. Sister Maria of Agreda, however, was never canonized, although her cause has been proposed to the church's Congregation for the Causes of Saints many times. Her biographers have said that while her body levitated surrounded by a blinding white light in her small cell in the convent, she experienced herself soaring on the wings of angels across the ocean and in space to what Spain called "the New World."

I had never had occasion to think of levitation as a reality, but Tyler had—although not with respect to Catholic saints. Within the UFO literature, levitation was a common theme. People reported that during a UFO contact event they had been levitated out of their beds into crafts, through windows, and so forth. Tyler proposed to come with me to Rome. The plan he suggested was that I would translate the documents and he would offer his analysis based on his work in aeronautics. Strangely, there was precedent for such collaboration. A number of individuals from aeronautic agencies had contacted me about my historical work on levitating saints. A colleague whose work focuses on Joseph of Cupertino had also been contacted by someone with similar space-related affiliations. Apparently, at least some members of the space industry believed in the possibility of levitation.

Tyler and Maria were, in a sense, inadvertent colonists in their respective eras, who made imagined "first contact." Maria allegedly bilocated to New Mexico, and the stories of her experiences helped Spanish missionaries obtain funding to convert indigenous Americans. Tyler was at the forefront of human efforts to colonize space. Just as Maria's voyages through space and to New Mexico preceded and accompanied Spanish missionaries, Tyler's mental landscapes—which included the creation of alien-based technologies—were supported by a massive media infrastructure of UFO content, a fertile context for efforts to colonize and populate space. Maria's case is similar to Tyler's in that she seeded the cultural imagination with supernatural support for the missionaries' work.

TYLER'S SPIRITUAL EXPERIENCE: NOTES FROM THE FIELD

It is one thing to describe how people utilize a UFO–biblical or religious–UFO framework for understanding how their religious traditions are linked to the new UFO mythos. It is another thing entirely to see it taking place. Being witness to the transformation of an individual's religious belief and practice is a powerful experience. I have witnessed this transformation more than once. Christopher Bledsoe, a Baptist from North Carolina, had been a pilot and owned a successful construction business. He had a profound UFO sighting that he interpreted as an extension of his own religious tradition. His congregation rejected his interpretation and called the experience demonic. For Bledsoe, this was an agonizing process that alienated him from his community and changed his life. Bledsoe struggled for several years, although he now seems at peace with his conversion. Tyler's experience was an accelerated version that happened dramatically during his visit to the Vatican and the observatory at Castel Gandolfo.

I began to suspect that this would not be an ordinary experience as I observed how Tyler was admitted to the Vatican Secret Archives. Gaining entrance to the archives is not easy, and I had started the process a year before my trip. The archives extend underground, and there are approximately fifty-three miles of shelving. One cannot just "request" a manuscript, because the archivists must find out where the manuscript is housed and then retrieve it, which is often a lengthy process. I provided the archivists as much information as I could prior to my visit. One needs particular credentials to enter the archives, which are called "secret," from a Latin word that should more accurately be translated as "private." I had the requisite credentials: I have a PhD and am a tenured professor in religious studies, specializing in Catholic culture. There was a question about whether Tyler would be admitted. He is a respected scientist with over forty patents to his name, but he did not have a PhD, nor was he in any way associated with religious history.

Tyler arrived in Rome a day before me. I was in transit when he began sending me a series of texts. He was at the archives, but he was not allowed to enter. He had hired a translator who was dickering with the security personnel and explaining that I had given him permission and needed his help. The archivists knew I would be arriving shortly but said that Tyler did not have the proper credentials and would not be admitted. There were three stations of security through which one had to pass before obtaining a badge of entry. He was being held at the first station. Tyler had credentials as an adjunct instructor at several research universities and letters from the deans of those universities. He had a letter from me vouching that he was an analyst necessary for the project. None of this seemed to matter, and I sensed Tyler's resignation. There was nothing I could do, as I was on a plane thirty thousand feet above the Atlantic Ocean.

Tyler texted, "Should I tell them who I am?" I considered his question carefully. Why would it mean anything to them? And if it did, that might make things worse for us. I cautioned him against doing it, as I thought it wouldn't help and would possibly flag us as suspicious. We were there to view centuries-old documents about levitating saints. As a scholar of religion, I wouldn't raise any red flags of suspicion whatsoever. But Tyler's work in aeronautics certainly would. I said "no." But eventually it was apparent that he would not be admitted at all. At that point, after almost two hours of Tyler's translator haggling with security, I thought it couldn't hurt, so I said, "Okay, go ahead." The next text I received said, "I'm in. My archive badge is good for six months." Six months is the longest time for which one can have a badge. Tyler became, at that point, visible, at least to those at the Vatican Secret Archives. And his visibility provided access. Apparently, Tyler was known to members of the Vatican.

Things were still not easy. Tyler, now in the Vatican Secret Archives, was lost, and I was still in transit. He didn't know what he was looking at, or for. I had given him directions, but he doesn't speak Italian, and he was nervous and lost. Then he heard an American accent and saw a tall black-robed priest speaking in Italian with one of the archivists. He walked up to the priest and asked for help. The priest, Father McDonnell, could see that Tyler was lost and in need of help. He asked him to come outside into the courtyard. There Tyler explained what he needed to do. Impressed, Father McDonnell vowed to help. It turned out that Father McDonnell was a special person, known by seemingly everyone at the Vatican, and had access to its every nook and cranny. By the time I arrived in Rome, Father McDonnell and Tyler were fast friends. Father McDonnell had given Tyler rosary rings and Catholic prayer cards and asked him to pray. Tyler was a Baptist, so I had to explain to him what these objects were and what they meant. They were sacred objects for Catholics, beads and rings that helped them remember the reality of the sacred. Tyler told me later how, in the courtyard of the Vatican, with the sun streaming down on them, Father McDonnell had blessed our project. I was dumbfounded. Why? I wondered, as I watched Tyler try on the ring.

As it turned out, Tyler's unexpected access helped me too. Because of my association with him, I was able to look at documents and speak to key postulators (functionaries who present a case for an individual's canonization or beatification). This would not have happened had I been there alone. This point was further driven home by my interactions with the cadre of young archivists who manned the desks. Intimidating in their black robes, they spoke to Tyler instead of me, referring to me as "the lady doctor." Father McDonnell was not like the Vatican archivists. He was funny and easy-going, and spoke to me directly. He was fascinated by our research and curious too, as I didn't tell him exactly what I was studying. The study of the UFO phenomenon, from any angle whatsoever, is controversial, even if one is just approaching it as cultural history. I wasn't going to tell him that I was assessing accounts of levitation and bilocation with my space engineer colleague. At some point he figured it out, but it didn't affect his relationship with us, as he invited us to attend a Mass in St. Peter's Basilica.

The Vatican has traditionally been protected by the Swiss Guards, mercenaries who are trained by the Swiss Armed Forces. In their colorful attire, outfitted with swords, they are placed in strategic positions around the Vatican. They don't appear to provide any type of security. Their presence seems to be more for the benefit of the constant lines of tourists who circle the Vatican and stop for photographs. The real guards wore camouflage uniforms and carried very big guns, which looked like automatic weapons. The guns matched the gravity of their grim faces. They were everywhere. Against my counsel, Tyler asked one if he would like to have a cafe latte, to which the guard replied with a steely "no." To enter the Vatican grounds, we needed to pass by these formidable armed men. Fortunately, Father McDonnell, with his black robe and breezy demeanor, parted the guards like Moses parting the Red Sea, and as long as we were close behind him, we could go seemingly anywhere.

The second day of my visit to Rome I was in St. Peter's Basilica hearing Mass with Father McDonnell, Tyler, and six nuns. The Mass was celebrated in Latin, near the incorruptible body of Pope John XXIII, which certainly enhanced the surreal quality of my experience. We had passed by the grim-faced guards and into the sacristy, a chamber that seemed off-limits to all non-Vatican insiders. The priests were robing for the service. I carefully avoided direct eye contact with them. I could see that Tyler and I were conspicuous, judging by the many faces that turned in our direction.

When Father McDonnell was robed, we went back into the basilica, and the Mass began. I tried to help Tyler understand was what happening. I saw by the way he looked around at the frescos on the cavernous ceilings and the sunlight shining through the stained glass that he was in another world. I pointed out that before us was the incorruptible body of a saint, and he nodded in recognition. Later I found out that he didn't know what I had said and was astonished that we had been so close to a dead body. He had never heard of the tradition of incorruptible saints, according to which certain people's bodies do not decay after death and are pronounced "incorruptible" by the church. Most often these persons are considered by Catholics to be saints. Their bodies are often placed in glass cases, to be viewed by the faithful. Tyler and I talked about this on the day after his mother's funeral, two weeks after we had returned from Rome. The fact that we had been so close to John XXIII's preserved body was comforting to him.

After Mass, Father McDonnell invited us to follow him on rounds at the local hospital where he was celebrating another Mass, at a small hospital chapel, and administering last rites to dying patients, as well as anointing the sick. The last rites provide absolution for sins, preparing the dying person's soul for death. The anointing of the sick is one of the seven sacraments of the church, in which a priest blesses a person through the administration of blessed oil. I thought that Tyler's experience with helping terminally ill children would have prepared him for this. Before Mass, Father McDonnell and I recited several traditional Catholic prayers. Tyler, not knowing the prayers, sat in silent contemplation, looking around at the very small chapel, which contained a relic (a fragment of a bone) of St. Teresa of Avila. After Mass we went around the hospital with Father McDonnell. He respectfully announced his presence to the patients, and

those who wanted his services welcomed him. I was to accompany him to the bedsides of women, and Tyler was to
do so when it was a man who was dying. Father McDonnell
and I entered the room of a woman who seemed near death.
Her daughter sat beside the bed and held her mother's hand.
Father McDonnell's eyes shone with mercy and love as he
tenderly crossed the mother's forehead with blessed oil, and
he asked God to bless her. The old woman's eyes sparkled and
she smiled. I felt my throat constrict, and choked back tears.
As we left the room, Father McDonnell and I looked at each
other. He was clearly touched. He said, "Now you see. I get
more from them than I give to them. In there, was beauty. It
was God."

Tyler went with Father McDonnell into the room of a
young man in his late twenties or early thirties. I had seen
this young man earlier, at Mass. He had struggled slowly
with a walker to attend the service. He seemed like a proud,
strong young man who was humbled by the approach of
death. I could see that Tyler felt an immediate kinship with
him. Fifteen minutes went by, and then Tyler and Father
McDonnell came out. Tyler could not look at me. His head
was bowed. I did not try to speak with him, because I understood. His heart was broken.

This experience prepared Tyler for his conversion. As if
following a script, events happened one after another that
instigated a profound shift in Tyler's understanding of his
life and his future and of the reality of the beings. I was the
witness to these events, and to his transformation.

The day after the hospital experience we played tourist.
I thought that perhaps some sightseeing would lighten the
intensely religious mood that seemed to have gripped Tyler
since his first day in Rome. I was wrong. We took a tour

of Rome on a golf cart, which turned out to be a bad idea. The streets of Rome are not smooth, and we jostled violently about as the tour guide steered our cart in and out of throngs of speeding trucks and vans. At one point, we were pulled over by the police. The guide and the police haggled for twenty minutes. We waited patiently and were finally brought to the beautiful church of Santa Sabina, which is the oldest remaining Roman basilica and sits atop the Aventine Hill. The church is named for a noble Roman woman who was converted to Christianity by her servant Seraphia. Both were executed by the Roman government and later declared saints. The church was built on what is said to have been the site of Sabina's home, which was near a temple of the goddess Juno. The place was steeped in Roman and Roman Catholic history.

Tyler and I made our way around the church as the guide described the history of the location and its significance to Italians. We happened to arrive just as a wedding party was making its preparations. A small group of classical musicians was playing as we toured the church. Tyler found his way to a small side chapel. Was he kneeling? I couldn't tell, as a crowd of worshippers obstructed my view. At that moment, the guide happened to meet a friend, a historian of that church who had just finished giving a tour. The historian led me outside of the church and showed me its large wooden door. On the door was carved one of the earliest depictions of the crucifixion of Christ. He is pictured as if standing calmly with outstretched arms, between the two thieves, whose arms are also outstretched. They looked expectant, not crushed or tortured. But this was not all that was on the door. I also saw images of levitation. I was struck by these images and asked the historian about what they depicted, and she seemed confused.

"I suppose, yes, these are of levitations," she said.

The ascension of Christ is depicted in two panels, and then a third shows Christ ascended. Beneath him is a mysterious object that looks like a globe or disc—scholars are not sure what it represents. Later, as I researched the mystery object, I found several websites that associated it with a UFO. Another panel represents the prophet Elijah ascending into the heavens on a cloud, and in yet another panel the prophet Habakkuk is either ascending to heaven or being lifted up by an angel. Overall, the door showed numerous examples of bodies ascending to the heavens.

I was excited to share my discovery with Tyler, but when I searched for him in the church, he was nowhere to be found. I found our guide and asked her if she had seen him. She looked at me oddly and pointed toward the small chapel. There was Tyler on his knees, praying. The wedding guests were starting to arrive; we needed to leave. I looked at Tyler and realized that he was not in a normal frame of mind. I touched him and whispered that we needed to leave. The music was playing. The arriving guests were impeccably dressed, and several looked at us as if we were intruders. It was time to leave, yet Tyler was crying. Our guide, now very confused, explained that there was one more destination on our tour. We got back into the golf cart and left the church of Santa Sabina.

After the tour was over we found a quiet restaurant and ate a light meal. Tyler was quiet.

"Is everything okay?" I asked.

"No. Nothing's okay."

"What's wrong?" I asked, but I think I knew already.

"Diana, I have to go back and help people directly. I feel like I am a complete failure."

I was surprised, because Tyler is far from a failure. But now he felt like one.

"Will you help me?" he asked. "Will you introduce me to priests or nuns who can help me serve like this? I want to help anyone who is hungry or in need of help. I don't care if I ever work at my day job again."

"I will," I said.

I knew that Tyler was having a spiritual conversion, and that its effects in his life would be completely different from what he expected. I had a feeling that he would learn more about what the future held for him when we went to the observatory archive in Castel Gandolfo.

I was feeling very uneasy. To me the Vatican looked like a medieval feudal palace. The constant presence of the elite guards put me on edge. I understood that I was lucky that Tyler had met Father McDonnell and that we were then invited to attend several important meetings, but this was only because of Tyler's access. None of this would have happened had I been there alone.

As it turned out, our time at the Vatican Observatory couldn't have been more different from our experience at the Vatican. Brother Guy Consolmagno, director of the observatory, is a well-known astronomer who specializes in meteorites and asteroids. He is an American Jesuit with degrees from MIT and the University of Arizona. After we drove up to the observatory and parked, Brother Guy greeted us warmly. He gave us a brief tour of the premises, carefully showing us which doors we could enter and which were off-limits. After the tour, Brother Guy presented me with the keys to their archive. I have spent half of my life looking through archives—and this was unprecedented. Archivists are usually very protective of their holdings, and we were going to be looking at the works of Johannes Kepler and other great scientists of Western cosmology. When Tyler saw the list of books we would be viewing, his face lit up. He had spent his entire life exploring space, and now he would get to see the original works that had paved the way for his present vocation.

The archive itself is beautiful. On exhibit are old technologies of space exploration: the first telescopes developed to scour the galaxy. Brother Guy had lined the walls with old photographs of nuns who had worked at the observatory and helped to chart star patterns. He was correcting the historical record by including those who had been left out of it. I felt like I was home, and Tyler did too.

Every morning, around 10 a.m., the brothers and priests would gather for cappuccino and cafe latte in a room near the archive. As anyone who has been to Italy can attest, Italian coffee may be the best in the world. Tyler, who used to avoid coffee as part of his healthy living protocol, had cast aside restraint and was now addicted. We stood in a small room with about ten Jesuits with various types of PhDs, all connected to space in some way—astrophysics, astronomy, and related disciplines.

"What are you looking for in our archive?" one of the brothers asked.

I wasn't going to say that I was writing a book about the topic of UFOs. That could have immediately alienated us from these amazing scholars. I told the truth but without using the word "UFO."

"We are looking for instances of aerial phenomena."

"Aerial phenomena?" Several of the others stood and stared at us.

"Yes."

I waited a few seconds, and then I laughed. To my relief, they laughed too. That was the end of the conversation.

To set the record straight, the Jesuits at the Vatican Observatory are not actively searching for UFOs, nor are they engaged in anything related to ufology. Brother Guy has a wonderful sense of humor and some of his jokes and comments, taken out of context, have fed into conspiracy theories about the Catholic Church. What these scientists *are* doing is revealing that science is compatible with religion. And they are doing it so effectively that, after hearing Brother Guy speak about his vocation, my Baptist scientist colleague chose to become a Catholic.

TYLER'S TRANSFORMATION AND HIS REVISED UNDERSTANDING

On our first morning in the archive, Brother Guy stuck his head in the door and peeked in at us. We were busy identifying books we wanted to read that day. Brother Guy told us that he was heading up to the actual observatory where the telescopes were housed and asked if we wanted to come to a talk he was giving to a group of young scientists from the European Space Agency. Of course we did. I'd heard Brother Guy speak several times and I knew that his insights, which were always delivered with humor, could be profound and transformative. I had a feeling that this talk would influence Tyler, who was on fire to change his life. We jumped up from our desks and helped Brother Guy get organized for the talk. Soon we were in a car driving through the gardens of the estate and up to the top of the small mountain, which overlooked a crystal-blue volcanic lake. The first thing I noticed, besides the breathtaking scenery, was a fleet of sleek cars lined up in a row, gleaming in the morning sun. It was an impressive sight.

The young scientists were eager to see the historical hub of their own space program and to meet the Jesuit who directed this enchanting observatory. They were welcoming to Tyler and me when Brother Guy introduced us. I was introduced as a professor from the University of North Carolina; when Tyler was introduced, along with his affiliations, the youthful crowd burst into cheers and applause. I was proud that, at least among these smart young Europeans, Tyler, whom I considered an American hero, was not invisible.

As I predicted, Brother Guy's talk was funny, informative, and profound. He made the young scientists laugh and cry. He addressed the conspiracy theories about what he and the other scientists do at the observatory by showing images from popular culture, such as scenes from popular movies and books that paint Castel Gandolfo as a hub of mystery and intrigue, and then the reality, which turned out to be pictures of the priests and brothers sitting together discussing the composition of meteorites. The pictures conveyed the mundane daily lives of the observatory scientists, even if they did have Italian lattes. The popular depictions of Castel Gandolfo were so far removed from the reality that the whole group erupted in laughter. Brother Guy talked about how, after he received his PhD, he felt a call to help people in need and had joined the Peace Corp. Stationed in a very poor country, he helped to feed the people of the small town where he was posted and helped them obtain clean water. At night the villagers would gather together and implore him to take out his telescope so they could look up at the night sky. They asked him about the meaning of what they saw. It was then, he said, that something within him clicked. He realized that he had a vocation, and that was to help people realize that there is more to life than just what to eat for lunch. The wonder of the cosmos and the questions that arise from it were part of the human condition. It was as important as the bread we eat, as it fed the soul. It was literally spiritual food. He realized that he was in a unique position to help foster this wonder.

Brother Guy's words sent an electric charge through the audience. When he finished, everyone rose and filed into the observatory for a demonstration of the telescope. Tyler was introspective. I could tell that Brother Guy's talk had affected him the way I thought it would. Not only did Tyler have a desire to help people in a meaningful way, like Brother Guy, but also he had similar training and also worked in space-related research. He was touched by the wonder of the cosmos, and his life was a testament to a type of vocation not recognized by secular institutions. Here, at Castel Gandolfo, he saw that there were scientists who lived a life of vocation, or calling. They wedded their spiritual lives to their work lives. They didn't compartmentalize religion into attendance at a religious service one day a week. Their faith, spirituality, and religion permeated everything they did. And they were scientists.

That night Tyler and I were in the archive, looking at the first of the books by Kepler. I had noticed that the observatory's neighbor was a convent and the home of cloistered nuns, and my own room was adjacent to theirs. As I sat in the archive of the Vatican Observatory in Castel Gandolfo, staring at Johannes Kepler's analysis of Copernicus's cosmology, I was struck by the thought that Sister Maria of Agreda, whose records I had seen, had claimed to have bilocated to New Mexico, the part of the world where Tyler had taken James and me to visit the supposed UFO crash site. I looked up quickly. Tyler looked at me, surprised by the suddenness of my move.

"I was blindfolded on the trip to New Mexico," I said, "so I don't know exactly where I was. But we just read about Sister Maria and she describes where she went. Is this the same place where she imagined she went?"

Tyler's face appeared to freeze and he looked back down at his book. He wasn't going to answer me. The small archive suddenly felt large to me, not in any spatial way, but in a way that fused it with my memories of New Mexico.

SISTER MARIA OF AGREDA'S EPISODES OF BILOCATION

In the early 1600s, as Spain was exploring and colonizing western North America, the youthful Maria claimed that with the help of angels she flew through space and over the ocean to New Mexico. Her sister nuns said they witnessed Maria during her alleged bilocations and that she rose a few feet off the floor and was surrounded by brilliant light.

The veracity of Maria's account of her experiences was bolstered by reported encounters between Franciscan missionaries in New Mexico and members of a native tribe, the Jumanos, who presented themselves as eager to be baptized. Allegedly, the Jumanos said that they had been visited by a "lady in blue" who spoke to them about the Catholic faith.[1]

This story traveled back to Spain with Alonso de Benavides, the first commissioner of the Inquisition in New Mexico. He met with Maria and questioned her closely about what she saw and with whom she spoke. Benavides was impressed by her account, which included details of things of which he thought she could not have been aware, and he made a report to the king of Spain, Philip IV.

Maria's "journeys" were strategically politicized by Benavides. He and others used them to justify their continued funding and efforts to expand the Spanish empire. The missionaries wanted to believe, and most likely did believe, that Sister Maria actually appeared, in physical form, to the people who lived there. Benavides and others used this miraculous story as proof that God wanted this area under Spanish rule.

As I revisited this historiography, I thought about what was erased in its telling. Sitting in the archive, it was hard not to remember Sister Maria's early work on cosmography and her recognition of some of the "heretical" scientific discoveries of her own era. Those works, her first, were burned, and only a few copies remain. She wrote that she saw the earth from space, and it was a spinning sphere. She is best known as the author of the *Mystical City of God*, a biography of the Virgin Mary, and her earlier work on science and cosmography is largely ignored.[2] I could not help but draw a correlation with Tyler and his own imaginings of how humans will eventually explore and live in space. Was Tyler a contemporary Maria, existing in a sort of cloister of invisibility? Maria imagined herself traveling to what was for her a new world and making contact with its inhabitants, and this imaginary/real voyage paved the way for real missionaries. Tyler's visions are supported by television and media and we accept, on an "imaginary" level, Tyler's version of space travel. Maria's visions were spread through rumors, stories, and circulated letters. Today, visions of UFOs and space travel are fueled by a vast media industry.

Just as in Tyler's case, there were inexplicable realist aspects to Maria's imaginings. Had Maria been alive today, perhaps she would have been a remote viewer with the Stanford Research Institute, as she seems to have possessed the qualifications and skills. There is a history of psychic cosmonauts within religious traditions, people who claim to fly through space with the help of angels or beings of light. Even if Maria in some sense creatively imagined a place to which she had never been, but had perhaps read about, it would not discredit the very real history of how her reported travels helped legitimize continued Spanish expansion. As Jeff Kripal suggests, instead of positing an either/or scenario that negates the inexplicable and anomalous and reduces Maria's claims to purely imaginings and nothing more, why not consider the story within a framework of both/and? This would allow both the possibility that Maria really had some experiences that cannot be easily explained away or reduced to political machinations *and* that these experiences helped pave the way for Spanish colonization in a world that was new to them, a place where people had already existed for thousands of years.

Maria articulated her own version of the events and their inexplicable nature. She even criticized Benavides for being too "literal" in his interpretation of her bilocations. At the same time, she insisted that they *really did happen*. She wrote:

> God showed me those things by means of abstract images of
> the kingdoms and what was going on there, or perhaps they
> were shown to me there. Neither then nor now was, or am,
> I capable of knowing the way it happened. . . . Whether or not
> I really and truly went in my body is something about which
> I cannot be certain. And it is not surprising I have questions
> in my mind, for Saint Paul understood things better than
> I and yet tells us that he was carried up to the third heaven but
> does not know whether it was in the body or out of it. What
> I can assure you beyond any doubt is that the case did in fact
> happen, and that as far as I know, it had nothing to do with the
> devil or wrong desires.[3]

Significantly, Maria notes that her travels would not have
happened without the assistance of angels, or angelic beings.
Angelic beings show up, again and again, in the discourse of
the psychic cosmonauts. Of course, Tyler believes in beings
that help him develop technologies.

Empirical or not, Maria's imaginings helped Spain colonize part of America. As a woman living in the seventeenth
century who dared to write, she inspired suspicion and had
to answer to the Inquisition. She later claimed that she was
pressured to answer to Benavides in ways that he desired.
Some of her writings were burned. Later, she recanted her
recantations and rewrote many of her former works from
memory. Colonial expansion was forged through the energy,
money, and desires of the Spanish elite. Maria's voyages and
"first contact" were put in service to this end.

Across the table in the silent archive, Tyler was diligently
searching through the pages of an eighteenth-century book
about electromagnetism. I considered that his own special
skills were used to serve an industry that sought colonization
and expansion of space. It was also an endeavor undertaken

by the elite. The heads of the private space industries are billionaires, and ufology and the study of anomalous aerial phenomena, as observed by my colleague Brenda Denzler, are "overwhelmingly white and male" and over 90 percent Anglo-American.[4] To make it even more difficult to attain any kind of real knowledge about the topic, Tyler's work is invisible, as is most of James's. The historians of ufology, with few exceptions, ignore the history of African American and indigenous traditions of the UFO, which predate the standard assumption that the UFO mythos was born in the year 1947. The founders of the Nation of Islam were articulating a UFO narrative by the 1930s, and according to Elijah Muhammad, the religion's early leader, Wallace Fard Muhammad, had spoken of UFOs in the 1920s.

That night, Tyler admitted that his understanding of the "beings" was being transformed by his experiences. His encounter with Sister Maria and her alleged bilocations, the idea that they may have happened within a hub of modern UFO activity, and information about the levitations of other saints and even apparitions of the Virgin Mary had significantly affected his new understanding. This information, coupled with what he had felt while making hospital rounds with Father McDonnell, and then the insights he gathered from the other scientists at the Vatican and the Vatican Observatory, shifted his interpretive structure with respect to what he thought might be extraterrestrials. He felt more in touch with them than ever and that somehow his connection had been "supercharged" by the environment in Rome and in Castel Gandolfo, but he also felt that he knew less about what they were, who they were, and their intentions. Later that night we were sitting alone in the archive. Tyler was quietly looking through a manuscript. He received a text message.

He told me, as he slumped in his chair, that his mother had just been admitted to hospice.

Every night, the brothers and priests at the observatory celebrate Mass in a small chapel. We were always invited to attend. I now suggested to Tyler that we go, and he readily agreed. When we arrived at the chapel I asked the priest if he would offer the Mass for Tyler's mother. Tyler was touched. He asked the priest to bless some rosaries that he had bought in the Vatican.

During the last conversation he had with his mother after he returned home, he gave her a blessed rosary. She took it and put it around her neck and then held Tyler's hand. Later, before her funeral, he asked his Baptist siblings if they would allow their mother to be buried with the rosary. Seeing how moved she was to have received the gift, and knowing that the brothers and priests at the Vatican had prayed for her, they readily agreed. Later Tyler learned that, while the Mass was being celebrated in the observatory chapel, his mother, who had been uncommunicative for months, roused to consciousness for several hours with perfect memory and conversed with her family. This was reported to Tyler by his sister. She did not know that Tyler, and the observatory community, had been praying fervently for their mother during that time.

THE ENDING AND
THE BEGINNING

Tyler's life has been unusual by any standard, but it had not been overtly religious. He believed that he was in contact with beings of some sort, and that this contact was spiritual.

However, he never theorized about what the beings were, other than that they were related to spirituality and space. This trip motivated him to begin thinking about who the beings might be. He now felt a kinship to Sister Maria of Agreda, and he vowed to devote his life to a new ministry. He believed that these beings were, or were similar to, the beings spoken of by Sister Maria, the angels that had transported her to what is now the southwestern United States. Like Rey Hernandez, a confirmed atheist whose experiences transformed him into an agnostic, Tyler's understanding of his relationship to the beings shifted completely.

Months after we returned to the United States, Tyler was invited to return to Rome. He would make his first communion as a Catholic at a small Mass with Pope Francis, at none other than the church of Santa Sabina where he had first felt, in his words, the presence of the Holy Spirit. The Mass took place on St. Valentine's Day, which, in a rare occurrence, was also Ash Wednesday this year. I never anticipated that this story would end like this, with Tyler's conversion to Catholicism. For Tyler, it was not an end, but the very beginning.

CONCLUSION

The Artifact

Credo quia absurdum, eh, Diana?

—JACQUES VALLEE

IT TURNS OUT THAT ABSURDITY seems to have been written into the fabric of the artifact—that is, the artifact I had found with James and Tyler, or that was perhaps planted for me to find. It was analyzed by research scientists, who concluded that it was so anomalous as to be incomprehensible. According to these scientists, I was told, it could not have been generated or created on Earth. One scientist explained it to me in this way: "It could not have been made in this universe." This does not mean that the scientists believed it was created by extraterrestrials. They just did not know how, or by whom, it was made. They seemed comfortable, if amazed, with this degree of ambiguity. I recall something James told me about his research methods. He said that when his graduate students found data that did not appear to fit the hypothesis, they often ignored the data. He said that he would redirect them toward the anomaly. The anomaly, he explained, was there for a reason, and it was their job to understand why it was there, and then to possibly change their hypothesis. James and the other scientists had been presented with an anomaly. John Mack, during his own research with experiencers, had approached Thomas Kuhn, who had convincingly argued that scientific revolutions came about through attention to anomalies. Kuhn's advice for Mack was to focus on the raw data and to persist in collecting it, even if it did not fit into any preconceived or conventional frameworks of knowledge. This was precisely how the scientists were proceeding with their research.

To make matters more interesting, just before the holidays in December 2017, the *New York Times* published an article featuring the testimony of Luis Elizondo, the former director of the Pentagon's Aerospace Advanced Threat Identification Program, who alleged that the United States ran a secret program to study UFOs.[1] This article set off a firestorm of "disclosure" or "unofficial disclosure," which prompted public demands under the Freedom of Information Act that the US government provide any debris or "alloys" they might be keeping. Suddenly colleagues, including some who had scoffed at my interest in UFOs and the phenomenon, were now interested in the topic. The article promoted the "realism" that is one of the mechanisms of belief I elaborated on in this book.

As an object of mystery, the artifact functioned in religious ways, much like the relics of Catholic devotionalism or other religious traditions. The Shroud of Turin, which bears what appears to be the image of a man who had been tortured and crucified, is an example of a sacred artifact. The shroud is considered by millions of Christians to be the burial cloth of Jesus. As such, it is an object of devotion within the Catholic religion, although the owner of the shroud, the Catholic Church itself, has not pronounced it authentic. How the image originally got on the linen cloth *is* mysterious, and scientists and artists have tried to recreate medieval artistic and scientific techniques in hopes of showing that it could have been produced during that era, rather than at the time of Christ. None of the theories as to the origin of the image are conclusive. It remains a mystery. It is also an artifact of faith, devotion, and belief. It has its own history of being discovered and doubted, and it continues to leave a trail of miracles associated with it. Sacred artifacts are objects of power. Part of their power lies in their mystery.

Within the field of religious studies there are multiple definitions of religion, some of which consider the category of the mysterious. The term "religion" is common, but it is a slippery concept that has its own history and functions. When I explain religion to first- and second-year undergraduates, I explain that traditional religions usually have two main components. They contain functional aspects, such as places of worship like churches and synagogues, sacred texts, and oral traditions. These aspects of religion can be studied quite easily. There is also another aspect to religion—the "sacred" element. The sacred element is not easily studied, as it might involve a sacred event, or a *being*. It is the object of belief, but it is usually mysterious and cannot be studied, itself, objectively. One cannot put an angel under a microscope. It is this aspect, the mysterious sacred, that distinguishes religion from other organized practices like sports or fandoms. In religions, one finds the inexplicable, sacred event, or a mysterious artifact.

Tyler told me an anecdote that demonstrates the artifact's sacred significance to him and to many of the scientist-believers. Tyler had put the part in a backpack and had then stopped in to see a friend. He and his friend visited and dined, and then Tyler left to continue his travels. The next day he received a message from his friend.

"I had a dream about the contents of your backpack. I dreamt that there was a separate universe that you carried in it. A universe that was created within this universe that who knows where this universe was created. Had very much the essence of turtles all the way down . . . ha!"

Tyler asked me what I thought of his friend's dream. It was indeed an interesting dream considering what was in the backpack. I asked Tyler what he thought.

"Remember what Whitley [Strieber] told us? That the artifacts we studied also studied us? That is what I think is happening here," he said. "There is some sort of symbiotic relationship between the artifact and those in its proximity. It generates information. Some people are able to pick up on that information. Don't ask me to explain it, because I can't."

For Tyler and the scientist-believers, the artifact's mystery is not only impenetrable but also compels their reverence and belief. It inspires them. In the words of Tyler D., it was "elegant beyond comprehension." At the end of my research, I am an outsider to the community of scientists who are also believers. I can't solve the mystery of the artifact, but I have seen how its reality has inspired belief and, as Jung notes, rumors that spin mythologies.

The artifact and its influence on the scientists were disconcerting to me. I wasn't sure of its implications. I tended to think in terms of literal answers to its mysteries, for example, that it might be technology that belonged to another country. When I suggested this, the scientists looked at me incredulously. Apparently, they saw this line of speculation as among the least helpful of those that could lead to possible answers.

Even more disconcerting to me than the mystery of the anomalous artifact was the level of belief produced by media representations of UFOs. I saw media professionals use the mechanisms of belief to push a story that was at times very far removed from the event that inspired it, and yet it was believed by millions. It was this that was most concerning, as I came to understand the extent of the influence, and thus power, wielded by the media in regard to belief in UFOs and extraterrestrials.

Toward the end of my research for this book, as I sat in the Vatican Observatory archive, I had come across astronomer Carl Sagan's book *Intelligent Life in the Universe*. His coauthor was Soviet astronomer Iosif Samuilovich Shklovsky. As I opened the book, I was struck by Shklovsky's words: "The prey runs to the predator." This referred to the search for extraterrestrial life, of course. It suggested that if humans actually did meet such life, it might not be friendly. I came to understand these words in a different way. I related them to our relationship to media and technology and the unreflective embrace of both. As philosopher Martin Heidegger had predicted years earlier, technology would bring about a new era, an era as much dominated by technology as the medieval era had been dominated by God. Technology and its effects would be misunderstood. In this misunderstanding, Heidegger argued, humans would face a great and potentially very destructive crisis. In Heidegger's last interview, the German magazine *Der Spiegel* asked if philosophy could prevent such a negative outcome. Heidegger answered: "Only a God can save us now." At Heidegger's request, the interview was only published posthumously.[2]

NOTES

Introduction

1. Jon Austin, "Billionaire Helping Develop NASA Spacecraft Says Aliens Are Here-But It's Covered Up," *Express*, May 31, 2017, http://www.express.co.uk/news/weird/810957/Robert-Bigelow-60-Minutes-UFO-aliens-NASA-Bigelow-Aerospace.
2. Stephen Hawking, "Questioning the Universe," filmed February 2008, TED Talk, 10:12, posted 2008, https://www.ted.com/talks/stephen_hawking_asks_big_questions_about_the_universe#t-595954.
3. Jeremy Sconce, *Haunted Media: Electronic Presence from Telegraphy to Television* (Durham, NC: Duke University Press, 2000).
4. Massimo Teodorani, *Signal vs. Noise in Ufology*, personal communication, August 15, 2017.
5. Lee Speigel, "Eric Davis, Physicist, Explains Why Scientists Won't Discuss Their UFO Interests," *Huffington Post*, July 20, 2013, accessed September 10, 2017, http://www.huffingtonpost.com/2013/07/20/physicist-eric-davis-mufon-symposium_n_3620126.html.
6. Leslie Kean, *UFOs: Generals, Pilots, and Government Officials Go on the Record* (New York: Three Rivers Press, 2010).

7. "Most Say Humans Aren't Alone; Few Have Seen UFOs," Scripps Survey Research Center at Ohio University, http://newspolls.org/articles/19620.

8. Some examples include Barry Downing, *The Bible and Flying Saucers*, 2nd ed. (New York: Malrowe & Company, 1997), first published in 1968; and Michael J. S. Carter, *Alien Scriptures: Extraterrestrials in the Holy Bible* (Nashville: Grave Distractions Publications, 2013).

9. Jacques Vallee, *Messengers of Deception: UFO Contacts and Cults* (Daily Grail Publishing, 2008), appendix.

10. Carl Jung, *Flying Saucers: A Modern Myth of Things Seen in the Skies* (Princeton, NJ: Princeton University Press, 1978), 16.

11. Whitley Strieber and Jeffrey J. Kripal, *The Supernatural: Why the Unexplained Is Real* (New York: Penguin Random House, 2017), 3.

12. Whitley Strieber and Jeffery J. Kripal, *The Super Natural: A New Vision of the Unexpected* (New York: Penguin, 2016), 3, 5, 6.

13. Ann Taves, *Religious Experience Reconsidered: A Building-Block Approach to the Study of Religion and Other Special Things* (Princeton, NJ: Princeton University Press, 2009). T. M. Luhrmann, *When God Talks Back: Understanding the American Evangelical Relationship with God* (New York: Vintage Books, 2012).

14. Carole Cusack, "Apocalypse in Early UFO and Alien-Based Religions: Christian and Theosophical Themes," in *Modernism, Christianity and Apocalypse*, ed. Erik Tonning, Matthew Feldman, and David Addyman (Leiden: Brill, 2014), 339–353. James R. Lewis, ed., *The Gods Have Landed: New Religions from Other Worlds* (Albany: State University of New York Press, 1995).

Chapter 1

1. Brenda Denzler, *The Lure of the Edge: Scientific Passions, Religious Beliefs, and the Pursuit of UFOs* (Los Angeles: University of California Press, 2001). Edward U. Condon, "Condon Report,"

Scientific Study of Unidentified Flying Objects, 1968, http://files.ncas.org/condon/index.html. Robbie Graham, *Silver Screen Saucers: Sorting Fact from Fantasy in Hollywood's UFO Movies* (White Crow Books, 2015).

2. Denzler, *The Lure of The Edge.* Greg Bishop, *Project Beta: The Story of Paul Bennewitz, National Security, and the Creation of a Modern UFO Myth* (New York: Pocket Books, 2005). Mark Pilkington, *Mirage Men: An Adventure into Paranoia, Espionage, Psychological Warfare, and UFOs* (New York, NY: Skyhorse Publishing, 2010). Graham, *Silver Screen Saucers.*

3. George M. Young, *The Russian Cosmists: The Esoteric Futurism of Nikolai Fedorov and His Followers* (New York: Oxford University Press, 2012), 152.

4. Saucey Saucerton, "Remote Viewing, Looking Toward the Future of Humanity. Unlock Your Mind," filmed 2011, YouTube Video 01:15:21, posted January 15, 2015, https://www.youtube.com/watch?v=IBcQ8RDIe9w.

5. Bruno Latour, *Pandora's Hope: Essays on the Reality of Science Studies* (Cambridge, MA: Harvard University Press, 1999). Simone Natale, *Supernatural Entertainments: Victorian Spiritualism and the Rise of Modern Media Culture* (University Park: Pennsylvania State University Press, 2016).

6. Credit to Rose Rowson, "Repost or Die: Ritual Magic and User-Generated Deities on Instagram," in *Believing in Bits: Digital Technology and the Supernatural* (New York: Oxford University Press, forthcoming).

7. George P. Hansen, *The Trickster and the Paranormal* (Bloomington, IN: Xlibris Corporation, 2001).

8. Kary Banks Mullis, *Kary Mullis*, December 14, 2016, https://www.karymullis.com/index.shtml.

9. Grant Cameron, *Inspired: The Paranormal World of Creativity* (Winnipeg: Itsallconnected Publishing, 2017), 33. Brad Steiger and Shelly Steiger, *Real Encounters, Different Dimensions, and Otherworldly Beings* (Canton, OH: Visible Ink Press, 2014).

10. "Secrets of the Creative Brain," The Aspen Institute, published on July 18, 2014, https://www.youtube.com/watch?v=unAbERa0otY, accessed May 13, 2018.

Chapter 2

1. "Report of Scientific Advisory Panel on Unidentified Flying Objects Convened by Office of Scientific Intelligence, CIA: January 14–18, 1953," 19–20, http://www.cufon.org/cufon/robert.htm.
2. "Blue Book Archive: Supporting Serious UFO Research," last modified November 15, 2005, http://www.bluebookarchive.org.
3. "Report of Scientific Advisory Panel on Unidentified Flying Objects Convened by Office of Scientific Intelligence, CIA: January 14–18, 1953," 19–20, http://www.cufon.org/cufon/robert.htm.
4. Jose Herrera, *V-28: A Fox Co. 1st Platoon Story* (CreateSpace Independent Publishing Platform, 2001), and personal communication.
5. See chapter 3 of Jeff Kripal, *Authors of the Impossible: The Paranormal and the Sacred* (Chicago: Chicago University Press, 2010).

Chapter 3

1. "In the Field—Active Observers and Researchers Around the World," https://www.facebook.com/groups/scottbrowne/.
2. Scott Browne's mother's diary, personal communication, April 23, 2017.
3. I am indebted to Erica Lukes of UFO Classified for this information.
4. Carl Jung, *Flying Saucers: A Modern Myth of Things Seen in the Skies* (Princeton, NJ: Princeton University Press, 1978), 16.
5. Ibid., 18.
6. Ibid., 23.
7. The Library Angel is mentioned throughout Koestler's book *The Roots of Coincidence* (Portland: Vintage, 1973).
8. Diana Pasulka, "From Purgatory to the UFO Phenomenon: The Catholic Supernatural Goes Galactic," in *Religion: Super Religion,* ed. Jeffrey J. Kripal (New York: Macmillan, 2016), 375–387.

9. Teresa of Avila, *The Life of Saint Teresa of Avila by Herself*, trans. J. M. Cohen (London: Penguin Books, 1957), 210.

10. Barry Downing, *The Bible and Flying Saucers*, 2nd ed. (New York: Malrowe & Company, 1997). Michael J. S. Carter, *Alien Scriptures: Extraterrestrials in the Holy Bible* (Nashville: Grave Distractions Publications, 2013).

11. George P. Hansen, *The Trickster and the Paranormal* (Bloomington, IN: Xlibris Corporation, 2001); Jacques Vallee, *Masters of Deception: UFO Contacts and Cults* (Brisbane: Daily Grail Publishing, 2008).

12. Fiedrich Nietzsche, *The Gay Science*, trans. Walter Koffman, "Aphorism 277" (New York: Vintage Books, 1974) 223.

13. Leon Festinger, Henry Riecken, and Stanley Schacther, *When Prophecy Fails: A Social and Psychological Study of a Modern Group that Predicted the Destruction of the World* (Eastford, CT: Martino Fine Books, 2009).

14. "Kubrick: And Beyond the Cinema Frame," last updated 2015, http://www.collativelearning.com/2001%20chapter%202. html.

Chapter 4

1. Stephanie Schwam and Jay Cocks, *The Making of 2001: A Space Odyssey* (New York: Modern Library, 2000), 163.

2. Alex Ben Block, "5 Questions with George Lucas: Controversial 'Star Wars' Changes, SOPA and 'Indiana Jones 5,'" *Hollywood Reporter*, February 9, 2012, http://www.hollywoodreporter. com/heat-vision/george-lucas-star-wars-interview-288523.

3. Jim Blascovich and Jeremy Bailenson, *Infinite Reality: Avatars, Eternal Life, New Worlds, and the Dawn of the Virtual Revolution* (New York: William Morrow, 2011), 1–2.

4. Diana Walsh Pasulka, "'The Fairy Tale Is True': Social Technologies of the Religious Supernatural in Film and New Media," *Journal of the American Academy of Religion* 84 (2016): 530–547. See also "The Total Recall Effect: Techno-Human Hybridity and Degrees of the Posthuman," in *Posthumanism: Emerging Technologies and the Boundaries*

of Homo Sapiens, ed. Diana Walsh Pasulka and Michael Bess. Macmillan Interdisciplinary Handbooks (Farmington Hills, MI: Macmillan Reference USA, January 2018). Alison Landsberg, "Prosthetic Memory: *Total Recall* and *Blade Runner*," *Sage Journals: Body & Society* 1 (1995): 175–189, https://doi.org/10.1177/1357034X95001003010.

5. Pasulka, "'The Fairy Tale Is True.'"
6. Jeffrey Zacks, *Flicker: Your Brain on Movies* (New York: Oxford University Press, Kindle Edition, 2014), 92.
7. Ibid., 105.
8. Ibid.
9. Blascovich and Bailenson, *Infinite Reality,* 1–2.
10. "Science Indicators Biennial Report. Science and Technology: Public Understanding and Public Attitudes," National Science Foundation, 2002, www.nsf.gov/sbe/srs/seind02/c7/c7h.htm.
11. Alon Harrish, "UFOs Exist, Say 36 Percent in National Geographic Survey," ABC News, June 27, 2012, accessed March 15, 2015, http://abcnews.go.com/Technology/ufos-exist-americans-national-geographic-survey/story?id=16661311.
12. "Report of Scientific Advisory Panel on Unidentified Flying Objects Convened by Office of Scientific Intelligence, CIA: January 14–18, 1953," 19–20, http://www.cufon.org/cufon/robert.htm.
13. Ibid.
14. I've written about this, specifically about the irony of the term and its reference to the P. K. Dick short story, in "The Total Recall Effect."
15. Impossible Factual Production Company, accessed September 9, 2017, http://www.impossiblefactual.com/.
16. "More Than Just Science Fiction," *If Star Wars Was Real,* http://www.nirahlee.com/iswwr/index.php?option=com_content&task=view&id=4&Itemid=30.
17. Jakob Schiller, "What It'd Look Like if *Star Wars* Spilled into the Real World," *Wired,* October 24, 2014, http://www.wired.com/2014/10/thomas-dagg-star-wars/.
18. Mike Horn, "Death Star over San Francisco," YouTube Video, 2:40, posted September 15, 2008, https://www.youtube.com/watch?v=AfqDVP_0O0c.

19. Scott Thill, "Sci-Fi Satire Fuels Fanboy's Funny *Star Wars* Videos," *Wired,* May 13, 2009, https://www.wired.com/2009/05/sci-fi-satire-fuels-fanboys-funny-star-wars-videos/.

20. Personal communication, April 2014.

21. Carole Cusack, *Invented Religions: Imagination, Fiction, and Faith* (Farnham: Ashgate Publishing, 2010). John Lyden, *Film as Religion: Myths, Morals, and Rituals* (New York: New York University Press, 2003).

22. David Chidester, *Authentic Fakes: Religion and American Popular Culture* (Berkeley: University of California Press, 2005), 17.

23. Michael Bess, Diana Pasulka, *Posthumanism: The Future of Homo Sapiens*; Carole Cusack, *Virtual Religions and Real Lives* (Detroit: MacMillan References USA, 2018), 167–178.

24. Markus Altena Davidsen, "Fiction-Based Religion: Conceptualising a New Category Against History-Based Religion and Fandom," *Cultural Religion* 14 (2013): 378–395.

25. Krishnadev Calamur, " 'Definite Evidence' of Alien Life Within 20–30 Years, NASA Chief Scientist Says," NPR, April 8, 2015, accessed April 13, 2015, http://www.npr.org/blogs/thetwo-way/2015/04/08/398322381/definite-evidence-of-alien-life-within-20-30-years-nasa-chief-scientist-says.

26. Robert Orsi, "Abundant History: Marian Apparitions as Alternative Modernity," *Historically Speaking* 9, no. 7 (Sep/Oct 2008): 12–16.

27. David J. Chalmers, "The Matrix as Metaphysics," in *The Character of Consciousness* (New York: Oxford University Press, 2010).

28. Jeffery J. Kripal, "Better Horrors: From Terror to Communion in Whitley Strieber's *Communion* (1987)," *Social Research: An International Quarterly* 84 (2014): 897–920.

29. Andy Clark and David Chalmers, "The Extended Mind," http://www.nyu.edu/gsas/dept/philo/courses/concepts/clark.html, accessed May 8, 2018.

30. N. Katherine Kayles, *How We Became Posthuman: Virtual Bodies in Cybernetics, Literature, and Informatics* (Chicago: University of Chicago Press, 1999).

31. Susan Schneider, "It May Not Feel Like Anything to Be an Alien," *Nautilus,* December 2016, http://cosmos.nautil.us/feature/72/it-may-not-feel-like-anything-to-be-an-alien.

32. Collative Learning, "2001: A SPACE ODYSSEY Meaning of the Monolith Revealed PART 1 (2014 update)," YouTube Video, 7:57, Posted August 15, 2014, https://www.youtube.com/watch?v=MSo6s_xrj4c.

33. David Halperin, *Journal of a UFO Investigator: A Novel* (New York: Penguin Viking, 2011).

34. David Halperin, *Intimate Alien*, unpublished manuscript.

35. Ibid.

36. Robert A. Baker, "The Aliens Among Us: Hypnotic Regression Revisited," in *The Hundredth Monkey and Other Paradigms of the Paranormal*, ed. Kendrick Frazier (New York: Prometheus Books, 1991), 57.

37. Elizabeth Loftus, "The Fiction of Memory," TED Video, 17:36, Filmed June 2013, https://www.ted.com/talks/elizabeth_loftus_the_fiction_of_memory?language=en.

38. Annette Kuhn, Daniel Biltereyst, and Philippe Meers, "Memories of Cinemagoing and Film Experience: An Introduction," *Memory Studies* 10 (2017): 3–16, https://doi.org/10.1177/1750698016670783.

39. Alison Landsberg, "Prosthetic Memory: *Total Recall* and *Blade Runner*," *Body & Society* 1 (1995): 175–189, https://doi.org/10.1177/1357034X95001003010.

40. "'Alien Encounters' 1995—When UFOs Invaded Disney World (Part 1)," *David Halperin: Journal of a UFO Investigator*, https://www.davidhalperin.net/alien-encounters-1995-when-ufos-invaded-disney-world-part-1/.

41. SubscriptionFreeTV, "Lost Disney UFO Documentary Original Full Version—Alien Encounters," YouTube Video, 43:32, posted February 24, 2014, https://www.youtube.com/watch?v=z3yt1DJpbvk.

42. Ibid.

43. As transcribed by David Halperin, January 13, 2017, https://www.davidhalperin.net/alien-encounters-1995-when-ufos-invaded-disney-world-part-1/, from this video: https://www.youtube.com/watch?time_continue=553&v=WshFZcSva6o, accessed May 8, 2018.

44. "Evaluating Information: The Cornerstone of Civic Online Reasoning," Stanford History Education Group, https://

sheg.stanford.edu/upload/V3LessonPlans/Executive%20
Summary%2011.21.16.pdf.

45. Camila Domonoski, "Students Have 'Dismaying' Inability to
Tell Fake News from Real, Study Finds," NPR, November 23,
2016, http://www.npr.org/sections/thetwo-way/2016/11/23/
503129818/study-finds-students-have-dismaying-inability-
to-tell-fake-news-from-real.

Chapter 5

1. Jacques Vallee, *The Invisible College: What a Group of Scientists
Has Discovered About UFO Influence on the Human Race* (San
Antonio, TX: Anomalist Books, 2014), 153.
2. Ibid., 30.
3. For an overview of this development see Simone Natale,
*Supernatural Entertainments: Victorian Spiritualism and the
Rise of Modern Media Culture* (University Park: Pennsylvania
State University Press, 2016).
4. N. Katherine Hayles, among others, criticized the assumption
that consciousness could be downloaded or otherwise moved
into nonhuman containers in her book *How We Became
Posthuman*.
5. Vallee, *The Invisible College*, 2.
6. Ibid., 107
7. Ibid., 126.
8. Peter Horsfield, *From Jesus to the Internet: A
History of Christianity and Media* (Hoboken, NJ:
Wiley-Blackwell, 2015).
9. Vallee, *The Invisible College*, 29.
10. George P. Hansen, introduction to *The Trickster and the
Paranormal* (Bloomington, IN: Xlibris Corporation, 2001),
http://www.tricksterbook.com/Intro.htm.
11. Ibid.
12. William A. Christian, *Visionaries: The Spanish Republic and
the Reign of Christ* (Los Angeles: University of California
Press, 1999).
13. Vallee, *The Invisible College*, 154.

14. Joaquim Fernandes and Fina D'Armada, *HEAVENLY LIGHTS: The Apparitions of Fatima and the UFO Phenomenon*, ed. Andrew D. Basiago, trans. Eva M. Thompson (San Antonio, TX: Anomalist Books, 2007), 35.

15. Antonio Marion Martins, *Novos Documentos De Fatima* (San Paolo: Loyola Editions, 1984).

16. Vallee, *The Invisible College*, 142.

17. Ibid., 3.

18. Ibid., 197.

19. Diana Walsh Pasulka, "The Spectrum of Human Techno-Hybridity: The Total Recall Effect," in *Posthumanism: The Future of Homo Sapiens* (Detroit: Macmillan References USA, 2018).

20. Robert A. Wilson and Lucia Foglia, "Embodied Cognition," in *The Stanford Encyclopedia of Philosophy*, ed. Edward N. Zalta (Spring 2017), Stanford, California: https://plato.stanford.edu/archives/fall2011/entries/embodied-cognition/.

21. Matthew Field, "Facebook Shuts Down Robots After They Invent Their Own Language," *The Telegraph*, August 1, 2017, http://www.telegraph.co.uk/technology/2017/08/01/facebook-shuts-robots-invent-language/.

22. Gabriel A. Radvansky and Jeffery M. Zacks, *Event Cognition* (New York: Oxford University Press, 2014).

23. Andy Clark, *Supersizing the Mind: Embodiment, Action, and Cognitive Extension* (London: Oxford University Press, 2008), 131–132.

24. N. Katherine Hayles, *How We Think: Digital Media and Contemporary Technogenesis* (Chicago: University of Chicago Press, Kindle Edition, 2012), 94.

25. Jacques Vallee, *The Futurist* "Computer Conferencing" and *Journal of Scientific Exploration* 2, no. 1 (1988): 13–27, 1988 Pergamon Ras plc. Printed in the USA.

26. Jacques Vallee, "A Theory of Everything (else)," video presentation, TEDx Talks, published on November 23, 2011, https://www.youtube.com/watch?v=S9pR0gfil_0, accessed May 15, 2018.

27. Ibid.

28. Used with permission from Stephen Miles Lewis's Facebook page, September 6, 2017, edited for clarity.

29. http://nietzsche.holtof.com/reader/friedrich-nietzsche/the-gay-science/aphorism-277-quote_c375fcf90.html.

30. Jacques Vallee, "Thinking Allowed: Implications of UFO Phenomena," published on November 12, 2016, https://www.youtube.com/watch?v=7ETMzkhBQ6w, accessed May 15, 2018.

31. See Sheila Jasanoff, "Future Imperfect: Science, Technology, and the Imaginations of Modernity," in *Dreamscapes of Modernity: Sociotechnical Imaginaries and the Fabrication of Power*, ed. Sheila Jasanoff and Sang-Hyun Kim (Chicago: University of Chicago Press, 2015), 1–31.

32. Gaymon Bennet, "Synthetic Biology: The Digital Creation of Life," in *Posthumanism: The Future of Homo Sapiens* (Detroit: Macmillan References USA, 2018).

33. Ibid.

34. Nicole Yunger Halpern, *Quantum Frontiers: A Blog by the Institute for Quantum Information and Matter @ Caltech*, December 25, 2017, https://quantumfrontiers.com/.

Chapter 6

1. Susan Demeter-St. Clair, "Making Mountains Out of Mashed Potatoes: UFOs as a Parapsychological Event," in *UFOs: Reframing the Debate*, ed. Robbie Graham (London: White Crow Books, 2017), 165–178.

2. Rey Hernandez, personal communication, December 28, 2017.

3. Rey Hernandez, Robert Davis, Jon Klimo, Rudolph Schild, and Claude Swanson, "Contact with Non-Human Intelligence and the Quantum Hologram Theory of Consciousness: Toward an Integration of the Contact Modalities," http://www.experiencer.org/wp-content/uploads/2017/02/Contact-with-Non-Human-Intelligence-and-the-Quantum-Hologram-Theory-of-Consciousness-Toward-an-Integration-of-the-Contact-Modalities.pdf, accessed May 20, 2018.

4. Rey Hernandez's interview in *Skeptico: Science at the Tipping Point*, accessed February 26, 2018, http://skeptiko.com/260-rey-hernandez-supports-ufo-contact/.

5. Rey's narrative comes from his self-published account, *My UFO/ET Contact Spiritual Experiences*, Rey Hernandez, JD, MCP, PhD Candidate, Codirector and Cofounder of Foundation for Research into Extraterrestrial Encounters (FREE), as well as through personal communication with me.

6. Rey Hernandez, personal communication, December 13, 2017.

7. https://www.johnytube.com/watch/yt/7zSO3jE4l-M/edgar-mitchell-an-epiphany-in-space.

8. http://ascentmagazine.com/articles.aspx%3FarticleID=195&page=read&subpage=past&issueID=30.html.

9. The Quantum Hologram Theory of Contact with Non Human Intelligence by Reinerio Hernandez, JD, MCP, PhD Candidate, FREE Board of Director and Cofounder, 2016.

10. http://www.experiencer.org/a-dyadic-model-of-consciousness-by-edgar-mitchell-sc-d/.

11. http://www.csicop.org/specialarticles/show/ufo_research_is_up_in_the_air.

12. http://www.history.com/shows/hangar-1-the-ufo-files/about.

13. https://blog.oup.com/2016/11/beyond-earth-research-big-data/.

Chapter 7

1. Several scholars of Maria, including Barr, note that the image of the Virgin Mary was already a well-known trope within the American Indian communities, and they would have used the phrase "the lady in blue" to indicate her power.

2. Works that helped me understand Sister Maria of Agreda, other than the primary sources I consulted, include Juliana Barr, *Peace Came in the Form of a Woman: Indians and Spaniards in the Texas Borderlands* (Chapel Hill, NC: University of North Carolina Press, 2007); Clark A. Colahan, *The Visions of Sor Maria de Agreda: Writing Knowledge and Power* (Tuscan,

AZ: University of Arizona Press, 1994); Nancy P. Hickerson, "The Visits of the 'Lady in Blue': An Episode in the History of the South Plains, 1629," *Journal of Anthropological Research* 46, no. 1 (Spring 1990): 67–90; Mar Rey Bueno, "Missionary Strategy or Feminine Genealogy? The Treatment of the Roundness of the Earth, from Sor María Jesús de Agreda," *Pecia Complutense* 14, no. 27 (2017): 49–64; Marilyn H. Fedewa, *Maria of Agreda: Mystical Lady in Blue* (Albuquerque, NM: University of New Mexico Press, 2009).

3. Clark A. Colahan. *The Visions of Sor Maria de Agreda: Writing Knowledge and Power* (Tuscan: University of Arizona Press, 1994), 121.

4. Brenda Denzler, *The Lure of the Edge: Scientific Passions, Religious Beliefs, and the Pursuit of UFOs* (Los Angeles: University of California Press, 2001), 164.

Conclusion

1. Helene Cooper, Ralph Blumenthal, and Leslie Kean, "Glowing Auras and 'Black Money': The Pentagon's Mysterious UFO Program," *New York Times,* December 16, 2017, accessed March 4, 2018, https://www.nytimes.com/2017/12/16/us/politics/pentagon-program-ufo-harry-reid.html.

2. Martin Heidegger, "Nur noch ein Gott kann uns retten," *Der Spiegel* 30 (Mai, 1976): 193–219. Translated by W. Richardson as "Only a God Can Save Us," in *Heidegger: The Man and the Thinker,* ed. T. Sheehan (Chicago: Precedent Publishing, 1981), 45–67.

GLOSSARY

Experiencers: Experiencers are people who have sighted or who believe they are in contact with the phenomenon. They have been called "contactees" or UFO-abductees.

The Invisibles: The invisibles are people whose work requires them to remain invisible, that is, completely removed from social media and the internet.

Meta-Experiencers: Meta-experiencers are scientists I encountered during my interviews with experiencers. They were interested in the details of the experiencer's sightings and often would apply this information to their own work on technologies. I also call them "scientist-believers."

The Phenomenon: The term "phenomenon" is used interchangeably with the term "UFO"; it is a more accurate term than "UFO" in that it does not suggest that an object is of extraterrestrial origin. In common usage, "UFO" is synonymous with "extraterrestrial aircraft," and many of the researchers featured in this book do not assume that the objects are of extraterrestrial origin.

Religion: There are many definitions of "religion," a term that most people take for granted. It is a modern term and many cultures do not even use it as a meaningful category. For them, religion and culture life ways permeate one another. However, in the West and within the university, we use the term "religion," and I use James Livingston's definition: "Religion is that system of activities and beliefs directed toward that which is perceived to be of sacred value and transforming power." Within most religions there is the "contact event," which is usually a "hierophany" in that it is the perceived contact between nonhuman, nonanimal intelligence, usually in the form of a god, divine being, or revealed knowledge, and humans.

Technology: In a basic sense technology is applied knowledge, or knowledge used in a practical sense for specific purposes. In this book the issue of technology and technological discovery is revisited through the lens of the philosophy of Martin Heidegger and my own ethnographic research involving biotechnologists. I will utilize the works of N. Katherine Hayles and others that place technology in relationship with humans in a process of coevolution. The biotechnologists reveal Heidegger's philosophy of technology and the process of "thinking" in that technology is "revealed," and thus functions as a form of revelation for these specific communities.

INDEX